# HEARTLAND

LENNY RUSSO

# HEARTLAND

FARM-FORWARD DISHES
*from the*
GREAT MIDWEST

PHOTOGRAPHS BY TOM THULEN
FINE ART BY GEORGE MORRISON

BLP
BURGESS LEA PRESS
NEW HOPE, PENNSYLVANIA

ᏊᏉ
BLP

BURGESS LEA PRESS
NEW HOPE, PENNSYLVANIA
An affiliate of Running Press Book Publishers

*Burgess Lea Press donates 100% of our after-tax profits on each book to culinary education, feeding the hungry, farmland preservation and other food-related causes.*

www.burgessleapress.com

2   3   4   5   6   7   8   9   10

Printed in China by 1010 Printing Group Limited

*Art direction* Ken Newbaker
*Book design* Jan Derevjanik
*Photography* Tom Thulen
*Food styling* Alan Bergo and Betsy Nelson
*Design direction* Whitney Cookman
*Book production* Victor Cataldo
With a special thanks to Michael Jones

ISBN 978-1-941868-05-8
Library of Congress control number on file with the publisher

*This book celebrates the food of
North America's Heartland, a region
with some of the richest farmland and
most abundant, diverse fauna
and flora in the world.
The Heartland was also the home of
acclaimed Ojibwe impressionist
painter and sculptor
George Morrison (1919-2000),
whose luminous landscapes and
wood collages appear in these pages.*

**—LENNY RUSSO**

# CONTENTS

# FOREWORD

BY LYNNE ROSSETTO KASPER

It's an old line but a perfect fit: "If Lenny Russo didn't exist, we'd have to invent him." Lenny is a believer, one of those people convinced he can change the world with no hesitation about doing everything possible to make it happen. Long before terms like "food justice," "sustainable," "farm to table," "local sourcing," "foraging" and "nose to tail" were the calling cards of committed cooks, Lenny was living them. Take a look at his recipes to see what I mean.

One thing Lenny is not is easy. Our first meeting in the 1980's was one of those "Can you top this?" go-rounds so dear to two people who live and breathe the same subject.

The man was opinionated, stubborn and convinced he could go where few chefs had gone before – to local farmers, artisans and into the woods for his food. Mind you, this was the '80's, when a cook on the California coast (literally overlooking the ocean) achieved star chef status by proudly boasting that all his fish came from France.

On the flip side was Lenny and his questionable sanity. He'd purposely picked Minnesota to build his dream of a menu that would thrive on local ingredients and traditions. Minnesota – the place where they say if summer falls on a weekend, have a picnic, and the place nicknamed then, "the land of the bland."

You know how it turned out. You're holding a piece of Lenny's dream in your hand right now. He made the dream happen in his Heartland restaurant in St. Paul. Beyond Heartland is his constant work on food issues – from food deserts to servers' wages. We didn't have to invent Lenny; he came to us as a pure, one of a kind original.

*April 2015*
*St. Paul, Minnesota*

# SUSTENANCE:
## AN INTRODUCTION

BY LENNY RUSSO

I was born the son of Leonardo Russo and Anna Luciano into an Italian immigrant family in 1958. We lived in a small apartment above a deli called Fiore's House of Quality at 414 Adams Street in Hoboken, New Jersey. Fiore's was known, as it still is today, for the quality of its hand-pulled mozzarella. My brother liked to play on the large wheels of imported provolone while, as a toddler, I dodged mice in the apartment upstairs. If you go to Fiore's today, you can still find the proprietor, John Amato, behind the counter.

John was a high school classmate of my cousin Frank Alecci. Frank's mother, Firenze, and my mother were sisters. My mother was the last of nine children, and his mother was the first. Frank and I still like to visit Hoboken and Fiore's whenever we can, and the mozzarella is better than ever.

Not too much had changed in the "Mile Square City" from when my mother was born in 1929 to when Frank was born in 1938 to when I finally arrived on the scene. We still shopped at Biggie's Fish Market two doors down. The original 1910 location of Carlo's Bakery, now famous from the TLC series "Cake Boss," was also on Adams Street, and we always dropped by for Italian pastry to enjoy after Sunday meals of Italian wedding soup, pasta with meatballs and sausage and eggplant parmigiana. We visited Custoza's Bakery for bread, Bob the greengrocer for produce and my great uncle's shop for live rabbits, chickens and freshly laid eggs. If we were in a serious walking mood, we would get our fruits and vegetables from the pushcart belonging to my paternal great-grandfather Leonardo, whom I am named after. That was fine as long you could order in Italian.

Mom's father Carmine Luciano made his own wine in the basement of the family's brownstone from grapes he would purchase across the river in lower Manhattan. He grew wonderful things, including gorgeous tomatoes and figs, in his tiny backyard. Every year before the snow fell he would wrap the fig tree in newspapers and burlap sacks to protect it from the winter winds. I remember him grafting several types of stone fruits to the same rootstock just because he knew he could.

Life pretty much revolved around food, wine and family back then. Like Hoboken in 1958, not much has changed for me. My life still revolves around those things.

Back in 1976, I found myself in Florida, attending New College in Sarasota. New College was kind of like hippie school. There were no required courses and no grades.

As a student, I was responsible, with a faculty adviser, for designing my curriculum.

I began my studies in literature and philosophy, eventually finishing in clinical psychology and writing an undergraduate thesis positing a holistic therapeutic approach to affective mood disorders. Not surprising was the inclusion of the role of diet and nutrition. For me, all roads have always led to food.

Unfortunately, as that first year came to a close I found myself broke. The idea of borrowing money as a way to continue financing my education was abhorrent to me. I was now faced with a dilemma. How was I going to get back to college for my second year without mortgaging my future?

By this time, my parents were living in a suburb of Miami so I jumped on a Greyhound bus and headed for their new home, where I knew I could freeload for the summer. I distinctly remember my arrival. Over the course of the year my hair had grown thick and wavy and fell to my shoulders. I was wearing a pair of blue jean overalls, no shirt, flip flops and a straw hat to keep the Florida sun off my face. A pair of dime store sunglasses rounded out my ensemble. As I stepped off the bus I could see my parents waiting for me. My father was shifting back and forth as he surveyed the crowd in search of his prodigal son. I walked right up to him, and heard him ask my mother if she could see me anywhere. That's when she exclaimed, "He's right in front of you! Quick! Get him into the car before anyone sees him!"

At their house, I found an old bicycle in the garage. I pedaled to the first business that looked like it might entertain the idea of employing a long-haired college kid for the summer. It was a French restaurant with the grandiose name of Quintessence.

I talked my way into a dishwasher job. That wasn't too difficult given that washing dishes in a hot kitchen in the middle of a Miami summer was no one's idea of a stellar career choice. The chef tossed me an apron, and I went to work scraping the leftover swill from people's plates, running them through an old-fashioned dishwasher and scrubbing pots and pans. When I was finished, I would scrub and mop the floors. In between, I was dodging the advances of the chef as well as several of the waiters. All of that for the federal minimum wage of $2.30 an hour. Even so, I considered myself lucky.

Of course, I knew I didn't want to do that for long. I already had pretty good cooking chops since my mother, a fabulous cook and probably the most profound influence on me in all things culinary, had taught me so well that I had been cooking dinner for my family since I was ten years old. It wasn't beyond my hubris to wash the dishes as fast I could and then run down to the garde manger station where I would assist in the preparation and plating of first course menu items and desserts with exotic names like Baked Alaska and Profiteroles.

*In St. Paul's Lowertown neighborhood, Heartland serves regionally sourced ingredients in made-from-scratch dishes.*

One day, the volatile owner and the garde manger got into one of their weekly shouting matches in the parking lot behind the restaurant. After taking a few futile swings at each other, the owner fired him, whereupon he burst into the kitchen demanding to know if anyone knew how to perform the garde manger duties. I proudly stepped forward.

Along with my new duties as garde manger came a pay raise. I was now working six nights a week for the incredible salary of $160, and was feeling pretty good about myself by the end of the summer, when I was prepping the entire menu including sauces, while still holding down my garde manger duties.

By early September, I had saved enough money to resume my studies. But now I had a new skill and the credentials to back it up. Since the student-faculty ratio at New College was 7 to 1 in 1977, I was able to create an academic program entirely comprised of tutorial work. Consequently, I could work in a restaurant kitchen beginning in midafternoon, study all night when I got off work and meet with my professors in the morning. Then I could go home, eat dinner, catch some winks and do it all over again. The way I had it figured, I was paying for one education while being paid to pursue another.

*Heartland and its adjacent market favor small family farmers and local artisanal producers over mainstream food purveyors.*

My usual employment regimen in those days was to seek out the best chef in the finest kitchen in town. Once I'd talked my way in, I would start at the bottom of the brigade and work my way up until I could progress no further. Then I would resign, go across the street or around the corner to a competitor and begin the process anew. I gained a reputation as an expert saucier, butcher and line cook by the time I was 20 years old. I thought I was pretty hot stuff, and I never had to borrow more than $350 the whole time I was in college.

I spent the ensuing years juggling two professions, working as an adolescent psychotherapist specializing in crisis intervention counseling and group and family therapy while continuing to cook at friends' restaurants and catering private parties. I knew I would eventually have to choose one profession over the other. The choice was not difficult. I was so much happier in the kitchen. So I resigned my position at the hospital where I worked and set about deciding where to refocus my career as a chef.

I remember vividly the conversation I had with my mother when I called to tell her about my decision to become a chef. She said, "That's not a real job." I told her that I was going to work for a guy named Paul Palermo and his father in St. Augustine Beach,

Florida. I explained that Paul was a friend of Wolfgang Puck, and he had helped Puck open his new restaurant, Spago, in Los Angeles. She had never heard of Puck. I told her not to worry about it. "He's from Austria," I said. I was pretty sure I could hear her blood pressure rising. I tried to explain that if I was ever going to be a serious chef, I needed to refine my method and technique, and was prepared to make the sacrifices necessary to do that. She was not convinced.

I had had enough of Florida. I exhaustively researched the best place for a young chef with no formal culinary training whose cooking was informed by his commitment to locally grown and sourced foods, and I settled upon the Twin Cities of Minneapolis and St. Paul. The combination of a vibrant economy in a state committed to preserving its natural resources and a cosmopolitan metropolis in close proximity to vast expanses of rich farmland was the deciding factor in making my choice. There was also a girl involved. I remember Old Man Palermo's reaction when I told him I was quitting in order to move to Minnesota. He looked me dead in the eye and said, "You're out of your fucking mind."

---

On Labor Day, 1985, I arrived in Minnesota, excited about the possibility of creating menus that celebrated the bounty of North America's Heartland.

After leaving Florida and passing from state to state, the swamps and bayous of the south had given way to the Great Smoky Mountains, eventually flattening out to the plains and prairies of the Midwest. I was astounded by the magnificence of America's agricultural might. I couldn't wait to arrive in Minnesota and partake of the edible largesse of its fields, forests and lakes. Boy, was I in for a shock.

I was surprised to learn that most chefs were not only failing to avail themselves of the incredible larder right outside their back doors, but they seemed totally unaware of it. Instead, they were importing most of their food from California and elsewhere, cooking what they perceived to be classical French and Italian fare. To my mind, they were ignoring the great cultural traditions of the Native American people, as well as the rich and varied farmhouse cooking of European immigrants who settled in the Midwest.

I set about learning as much as I could about Midwestern fauna and flora while forging relationships with small family farmers who were willing to supply me with ingredients directly from their land. My intention was to create a new cuisine with foods foraged from the forests and prairies, harvested from the lakes and rivers and cultivated in local farms and fields.

It took me two years to achieve that goal, and in 1988 I rolled out my first menus honoring the best ingredients I could find in Minnesota, Wisconsin, Iowa, the Dakotas, Michigan's Upper Peninsula, Manitoba and Ontario. It was also around that time that I had my first appearance in Food & Wine magazine, whereupon my mother admitted grudgingly, "Well, maybe cooking is a real job." Since then, my Midwestern provincialism has extended south and east to include lower Michigan, Illinois, Indiana, Ohio, Missouri, Nebraska and Kansas.

I became a standard bearer for what is now known as North American Midwestern Regional Cuisine, working only with ingredients from sustainable sources. I also made a commitment to social and economic justice by setting living wage standards for employee compensation.

In October, 2002, my wife Mega and I opened our own restaurant in St. Paul. Both the concept and the name, Heartland, were never really up for debate. The principles by which we run our restaurant are the same as those by which we run our lives. The menu changes daily and employs indigenous and sustainably cultivated ingredients from the American and Canadian Midwest. Since sustainability is just as much about the people who live here as it is about the land, our farmers are paid fair trade prices.

At Heartland, we cook entirely from scratch utilizing only whole foods. We were fermenting our own vinegars and blending our own mustards long before that became the fashion. In season, we forage for wild edibles, and as people in our part of the country have always done, we begin each spring with an eye toward winter by resuming the yearly process of pickling and preserving, so we will be prepared for the months ahead when the only things that grow here are snow and ice. We specialize in the preparation of our own charcuterie, making sure that, head to tail, no part of our farmers' animals goes to waste.

Above all, we stand by this most important belief: People engaged in the business of providing food, whether they are chefs, farmers or merchants, relate to others in the most fundamental way: we give them sustenance. With that comes a great deal of responsibility, and we take that very seriously.

I have the unique pleasure of giving joy to those who graciously allow us to serve them. We are often privileged to cook for some of the happiest times in people's lives: birthdays, anniversaries, graduations, job promotions and weddings. I can't really think of anything better than that.

# THE SPIRIT OF
# GEORGE MORRISON

BY KRISTIN MAKHOLM
DIRECTOR, MINNESOTA MUSEUM OF AMERICAN ART

The salt of the Minnesota earth, the ebb and surge of 10,000 lakes, the trees and rocks of the North Shore, and the great horizon over Lake Superior all give power and inspiration to the work of Ojibwe artist George Morrison. A native son of Minnesota and a nationally acclaimed modern artist, Morrison's work appears as a visual complement to this book because both his art and Lenny Russo's food are sustained and stoked by the Minnesota landscape.

Born in 1919 and raised near the Grand Portage Indian Reservation in Chippewa City, Minnesota, Morrison graduated from the Minneapolis School of Art and the Art Students League in New York City, where he embraced the style of Abstract Expressionism in the 1950s and 60s. When he returned to the Midwest in the 1970s to teach at the University of Minnesota, Morrison rediscovered his indigenous roots which infused paintings and sculptures resonant of the water, sky, trees, and horizon of Lake Superior. "People would say my forms are abstract," Morrison once wrote, "but to my own mind, they are offshoots from nature."

So it is with delight that the Minnesota Museum of American Art offers up these extraordinary artworks by George Morrison from our permanent collection as accompaniment to the rich tapestry of foods that originate in the natural world of Minnesota and the Midwest. Like the ingredients in one of Lenny's recipes, the pastel and wood, acrylic and ink in George's art combine to give substance to the spirit of Minnesota and meaning to the connection with our land.

**Spirit Path, New Day, Red Rock Variation: Lake Superior Landscape,**
1990, acrylic and pastel on paper, 22½ x 30⅛ in.

# SALADS
*and*
# STARTERS

In 1985, I started to create a new
Midwestern cuisine based on foods foraged
from prairies and forests, harvested from our
waters and cultivated in local fields.

# SALADS
*and*
# STARTERS

---

ST. PAUL FARMERS' MARKET SALAD • 23

FRISÉE AND SPINACH SALAD
with Warm Pancetta Vinaigrette and Poached Duck Egg • 26

FRESHWATER CRAYFISH AND SWEET CORN SALAD • 29

GRILLED PEACHES
with Toasted Walnuts, Greens and Chive Blossoms • 30

ROASTED BEET, FENNEL AND SWEET ONION SALAD • 32

MARINATED MUSHROOM SALAD • 33

BEEF CARPACCIO with Celeriac Salad • 34

CORNMEAL-CRUSTED OKRA with Sweet Corn Vinaigrette • 36

LAKE TROUT GRAVLAX
with Cucumber Salad and Dill Crème Fraîche • 40

MINT CURED RAINBOW TROUT
with Four-Parsley Sauce • 43

FENNEL-CURED WHITEFISH
with Danish Brown Bread Salad • 45

TURKEY RILLETTES
with Honeycrisp Apple Mustard • 46

MIDWESTERN COUNTRY PÂTÉ • 49

PICKLED CALVES' TONGUE • 54

WILD BOAR-TART CHERRY SAUSAGE • 55

THE ESSENTIAL BRAUNSCHWEIGER • 56

# ST. PAUL FARMERS' MARKET SALAD

This beautiful assortment of spring greens showcases the spring bounty of our area. I created it for the market located directly across the street from Heartland. The familiar greens suggested below provide a mere starting point.

More adventurous cooks appreciate the Asian ingredients grown by our local Hmong, Chinese, Vietnamese and Korean farmers who have cultivated small plots of land in and around Saint Paul. This recipe is meant to be adapted to use whatever greens are freshest in your area. I have never prepared it the same way twice.

| | |
|---|---|
| I cup basil leaves | 2 tablespoons grapeseed oil |
| I cup bias-cut chives | I tablespoon walnut oil |
| I cup chervil leaves | I tablespoon apple cider vinegar |
| I cup spinach or other sweet greens | I teaspoon sea salt |
| I cup dandelion or other bitter greens | 1/2 teaspoon freshly ground black pepper |
| I cup watercress or other spicy greens | |
| 2 dozen chive blossoms (optional) | |
| 1/2 cup walnuts, lightly toasted | |

Combine the basil, chives, chervil and the sweet, bitter and spicy greens in a large salad bowl. Sprinkle with the chive blossoms, if using, and walnuts.

Whisk together the oils, vinegar, salt and pepper in a small bowl. Pour the dressing over the greens, toss well and enjoy immediately.

# FRISÉE AND SPINACH SALAD
## WITH WARM PANCETTA VINAIGRETTE AND POACHED DUCK EGG

SERVES 6

This is Heartland's take on the classic French bistro salad *frisée aux lardons*.

We substitute duck eggs for the standard hens' eggs—look for them at your local farm market. Our house-crafted pancetta stands in for the lardons, or strips of fried pork fat, that typically grace this salad. I've lightened the dressing by substituting grapeseed oil for olive oil, and eliminating the Dijon mustard used in classic French vinaigrette.

White wine vinegar

6 duck eggs

4$^{1}$/2 cups (about 12 ounces) frisée, cleaned and trimmed

4$^{1}$/2 cups (about 12 ounces) spinach, cleaned and trimmed

3/4 cup Pancetta Vinaigrette, warmed

Heat a medium saucepan of water to boiling, and add a dash of white wine vinegar. Reduce the heat to a brisk simmer. Break each duck egg into a small bowl and slip into the water. Cook gently for 5 minutes. Remove from the water with a slotted spoon, drain and set aside.

In a large bowl, toss the frisée and spinach with vinaigrette to taste and divide among 6 serving plates. Top each salad with a poached duck egg and serve immediately.

## PANCETTA VINAIGRETTE

MAKES 2$^{1}$/2 CUPS

1 teaspoon sea salt

1 cup freshly squeezed lemon juice

2 tablespoons chopped garlic

1 tablespoon chopped shallots

2 tablespoons chopped flat-leaf parsley

$^{1}$/2 teaspoon freshly ground black pepper

1$^{1}$/2 cups grapeseed oil

$^{1}$/4 cup crumbled cooked pancetta

In a blender jar, dissolve the salt in the lemon juice. Add the garlic, shallots, parsley and pepper. On high speed, slowly add the oil in a thin stream until fully incorporated. Transfer to a small saucepan and stir in the pancetta. Taste and adjust for seasoning. Warm gently before serving.

# FRESHWATER CRAYFISH AND SWEET CORN SALAD

This sublime summertime salad combines fresh Minnesota sweet corn, recently husked and cut from the cob, with the delicate meat of our local freshwater crayfish tails. It's great when served alone as a first course, and even better when placed beneath a nicely grilled piece of fish. Fresh shrimp may be substituted for the crayfish.

I pound crayfish tail meat, cooked

2 cups fresh sweet corn kernels, blanched

1/4 cup coarsely chopped green onions

I teaspoon chopped flat-leaf parsley

I teaspoon chopped tarragon leaves

5 tablespoons grapeseed oil

2 tablespoons freshly squeezed lemon juice

I teaspoon sea salt

1/2 teaspoon freshly ground black pepper

In a large nonreactive bowl, combine the crayfish, corn, onion, parsley and tarragon. In a separate bowl, whisk together the oil, lemon juice, salt and pepper. Pour over the salad and toss gently to combine.

## THE MINNESOTA MUDBUG

Crayfish are the only native Midwestern shellfish worth pursuing. When they are in season, from July through early October, trappers gather freshwater crayfish in traps similar to those used by lobstermen along the Atlantic coast. In fact, crayfish look very much like miniature lobsters. They are somewhat tedious to prepare, but very delicious. You can find them already prepared and packed in their own fat in the freezer section of many Asian groceries.

At Heartland, we receive the crayfish live and process them immediately. First, we separate the tails from the heads, which are used to make shellfish stock. The tails are briefly poached in water with a bouquet garni and some lemons: we place the pot on the stovetop and wait for the water to boil. As soon as it does, we quickly drain the crayfish and submerge them in ice water. This is critical since they are very delicate and must not be overcooked. We then crack the shells of the chilled crayfish and remove the veins. During the season, we process anywhere from 25 to 50 pounds a week. The surplus processed tail meat and stock are frozen until winter when we use them in a variety of preparations, such as bisque and whole-grain risottos.

# GRILLED PEACHES

## WITH TOASTED WALNUTS, GREENS AND CHIVE BLOSSOMS

SERVES 6

In early summer we start getting crates of peaches from Michigan and southeastern Minnesota, where the local microclimate allows for cultivation of these juicy stone fruits. It's also a time of plentiful arugula and in our part of the country, the first tender leaves of spinach.

To dress this salad and heighten its riotous seasonal freshness, we infused an oil with fresh chives puréed in grapeseed oil, brought to a simmer and then strained. It is bright green and full of vibrant onion flavor. If everything comes together at just the right moment, the chives will also be flowering, and their purple blossoms provide a colorful, tasty garnish. Look for freestone varieties of peaches, which release their pits easily.

3 peaches, halved and pitted

I teaspoon grapeseed oil

1/2 teaspoon sea salt

1/4 teaspoon freshly ground black pepper

2 cups (about 6 ounces) arugula

2 cups (about 6 ounces) baby spinach, stemmed

1/4 cup walnuts, lightly toasted

6 tablespoons Chive Oil

3 tablespoons sherry vinegar

Chive blossoms, for garnish

Preheat a grill to high. Rub the peaches all over with grapeseed oil, and season with half the salt and pepper. Grill very quickly, flesh side down, for no more than 2 minutes or until tender but not soft. Slice 1/8 inch thick.

In a large bowl, combine the arugula and spinach. Add the walnuts and toss gently. Dress the salad to taste with the chive oil and sherry vinegar. Add the peaches. Season with the remaining salt and pepper and gently toss again. Divide the salad among chilled serving plates and garnish with the chive blossoms.

# CHIVE OIL

MAKES 1 CUP

We use this simple recipe to make a fantastic tarragon oil too. It's a great way to capture the flavor of fresh herbs.

¼ pound chives, coarsely chopped

¾ cup grapeseed oil

¼ cup extra virgin olive oil

Combine the chives and oils in a high speed blender and purée until the chives begin to disintegrate. Strain through a fine mesh sieve into a small saucepan and bring to a boil over moderately high heat, skimming any herb bits and fibers from the surface of the oil. Remove from the heat and strain again into a small bowl, then place immediately in an ice bath. Transfer to a jar with a tight-fitting lid.

# ROASTED BEET, FENNEL AND SWEET ONION SALAD

I use a lot of beets in my cooking. If you've ever spent a long winter in the upper Midwest, you understand why. Beets are among the vegetables that store well into spring while maintaining their freshness and flavor profile. A handy trick we use to extend that shelf life: when root vegetables start turning rubbery in the cooler, we store them overnight in a container of cold water. The roots absorb the water and are quickly rejuvenated.

This bright salad draws on the late summer and early autumn harvests of beets, fennel and sweet onions. It also uses the tarragon and chives that I find in my garden even as the leaves begin to fall. We ask the farmers we work with to plant lots of fennel late in the season, so we can continue to enjoy it as the summer begins to wane.

I pound beets, preferably a mix of Chioggia, white and/or gold

3 tablespoons grapeseed oil (divided)

I pound fresh fennel bulb, cored and thinly sliced

2 sweet or white onions, peeled and thinly sliced

2 tablespoons walnut oil

¼ cup walnuts, lightly toasted and coarsely chopped (optional)

I tablespoon apple cider vinegar

I teaspoon sea salt

½ teaspoon freshly ground black pepper

I teaspoon chopped chives

I teaspoon chopped tarragon leaves

Preheat the oven to 350°F. Cut the ends off the beets so they sit upright. Rub them with 1 tablespoon grapeseed oil and place on a baking sheet. Bake for 45 minutes, or until easily pierced with a fork. Allow the beets to cool until they can be safely handled but are still warm. Rub with a clean kitchen towel to remove the skins. Thinly slice and set aside.

In a large nonreactive bowl, combine the remaining grapeseed oil, fennel, onions, walnut oil, walnuts, vinegar, salt, pepper, chives and tarragon. Toss well, add the beets and toss again. Marinate for 15 minutes. Serve chilled or at room temperature.

# MARINATED
# MUSHROOM SALAD

This is a straight-up vegetable salad that uses mushrooms in place of greens—although of course mushrooms are a fungus, not a vegetable.

I prefer crimini or button mushrooms for this salad since they are meaty and readily available, but fresh porcini or king boletes would make fine substitutions if you are lucky enough to find some. They also make for a fancier, more upscale repast.

I¼ pounds thinly sliced button or crimini mushrooms

¾ cup cored and julienned fennel

¾ cup thinly sliced red onion

¼ cup apple cider vinegar

2 tablespoons sea salt

¾ cup grapeseed oil

¾ teaspoon freshly ground black pepper

2 tablespoons chopped flat-leaf parsley

2 tablespoons chopped tarragon leaves

Bring a large pot of salted water to a boil and add the mushrooms. Blanch the mushrooms for 2 minutes, then drain and let cool slightly.

Combine the mushrooms, fennel and onions in a nonreactive bowl.

In a separate bowl, whisk together the vinegar and salt, then incorporate the oil, pepper, parsley and tarragon. Toss the vegetables with dressing, making sure all the ingredients are well combined. Allow to rest for 20 minutes before serving. This salad does not like to sit overnight since the mushrooms will continue to weep and water down the dressing.

# BEEF CARPACCIO
## WITH CELERIAC

Some people might think that this recipe is all about the beef, but it was actually created to showcase the celeriac. Celery root, or celeriac, is commonly grown in Minnesota, and we have year-round access to organically grown roots of high quality. It takes a little effort to peel, but the flesh has a delicious, mild licorice flavor that works well in any number of preparations. It is one of our favorite vegetables at the restaurant.

12 ounces beef eye round, cut into 6 pieces and pounded very thin

Salt and freshly ground pepper

1¹/2 cups peeled and finely julienned celeriac

2 tablespoons chopped flat-leaf parsley

³/4 cup Horseradish Dressing

Divide the pounded beef among six chilled serving plates. Season with salt and pepper. Toss the celeriac and parsley with the horseradish dressing. Mound some of the celeriac on each plate and serve immediately.

## HORSERADISH DRESSING

MAKES 2 CUPS

It's important to taste and adjust for seasoning when making this dressing, since fresh horseradish varies greatly due to terroir and freshness. More salt and pepper might be needed if the flavor is flat. Generally speaking, however, very fresh horseradish root eliminates the need for much salt and pepper since the flavor is so assertive.

2 cups sour cream

¹/4 cup plus 1 tablespoon buttermilk

¹/4 cup fresh horseradish, peeled and grated

¹/2 teaspoon sea salt

¹/2 teaspoon freshly ground black pepper

In a medium bowl, combine sour cream, buttermilk, horseradish, salt and pepper. Whisk until well combined and taste for seasoning. Transfer to a container with a tight lid and refrigerate for up to 1 month.

# CORNMEAL–CRUSTED OKRA
## WITH SWEET CORN VINAIGRETTE

Crisp, succulent fried okra really sings when combined with bitter Japanese mustard greens in a summer corn vinaigrette. The natural mucilage in okra produces a thick, gelatinous substance when wet. By trimming the okra and soaking it overnight, I found I could use the mucilage as an adherent for the spicy cornmeal coating. I also like to combine fine and coarse cornmeal in a 50/50 ratio; the fine cornmeal adheres better, while the coarse cornmeal provides that crunchy texture I desire. Sunflower oil has a lightness that complements the nuttiness of the okra and sweet corn without overpowering.

**FOR THE SALAD**

4$^1$/2 cups (12 ounces) assorted Japanese mustard greens such as shungiku, tat soi and mizuna

1$^1$/2 cups Sweet Corn Vinaigrette

**FOR THE OKRA**

1 pound okra

$^1$/4 pound fine cornmeal

$^1$/4 pound coarse cornmeal

1 tablespoon cayenne pepper

2 tablespoons chopped flat-leaf parsley leaves

1$^1$/2 teaspoons sea salt

1 teaspoon freshly ground black pepper

Canola or grapeseed oil, for frying

In a large bowl, toss the mustard greens with the vinaigrette, starting with a few tablespoons and tossing until lightly coated. Divide among six chilled serving plates.

Trim the okra, cut off the tops and soak overnight in cold water.

When ready to cook, combine the cornmeals, cayenne, parsley, salt and pepper in a large bowl and mix until well blended. Scoop the okra out of the water with your fingers and toss it directly into the cornmeal mixture.

Heat at least 3 inches of oil in a deep fryer or large saucepan with high sides. Working in batches, carefully drop 6 okra pods into the hot oil. Turn to brown all sides evenly, 3 to 5 minutes. Using a slotted spoon, transfer the fried okra to drain on paper towels. Continue with the remaining okra. Season with a few pinches of salt and hold in a warm oven until ready to serve.

Arrange six pieces of Cornmeal Crusted Okra on each plate and serve immediately.

# SWEET CORN VINAIGRETTE

MAKES ABOUT 2½ CUPS

I teaspoon sea salt

2 tablespoons Corn Broth (page 276)
or vegetable broth

¼ cup champagne vinegar

I tablespoon minced garlic

½ tablespoon minced shallots

I tablespoon Dijon mustard

I teaspoon freshly ground
white pepper

1½ cups sunflower or grapeseed oil

I cup corn kernels, blanched

In a food processor, dissolve the salt in the broth and vinegar. Add the garlic, shallots, mustard and pepper. With the food processor on high, slowly add the oil in a thin stream until emulsified. Stir in the corn.

## WHERE THE OKRA GROWS

It may surprise you to find a recipe for fried okra here. I grew very fond of this edible member of the mallow plant family, and cousin of the hibiscus, when I lived in the South. On moving to Minnesota, I was intrigued to see northern-climate hibiscus specimens flourishing in botanical gardens. "Why couldn't we grow okra as an annual here in Minnesota?" I wondered.

I finally got my chance in the early 1990s when I became corporate chef for the Aveda Corporation. Its founder, Horst Rechelbacher, had opened a spa retreat in Osceola, Wisconsin, with an ambitious organic vegetable garden. By the time I arrived, the garden had fallen into disarray and was returning to weeds. I set about resurrecting it with the help of my friend Mac Graham. Among the crops we planted were several varieties of okra—and, just as I had suspected, the plants adapted well to the hot Wisconsin summer and the humid air that rolled up from the St. Croix River.

# LAKE TROUT GRAVLAX
## WITH CUCUMBER SALAD AND DILL CRÈME FRAÎCHE

The process of curing fish with salt, sugar and spirits is one of Scandinavia's most cherished contributions to the world of culinary arts. In times past, northern people cured their fish by wrapping it in birch bark and burying it for months before retrieving it, unwrapping it and digging into the putrid flesh. In fact, the word gravlax or gravlaks means "buried salmon." Today, curing fish is a relatively quick process that relies on autolysis, in which cells and tissue break down, resulting in a soft buttery texture that, while reminiscent of cooked fish, has a quality all its own.

Cured fish are best accompanied by copious amounts of aquavit. Ours is distilled and flavored in Illinois at North Shore Distillery. You'll find versions of it produced most anywhere Scandinavian immigrants have chosen to settle.

The recipes that follow require a fair amount of fish to execute properly. Cured fishes are meant to be shared, and it is a Scandinavian tradition to invite guests when it is served, or to give it away to friends and family. Note that it takes 8 days to cure the fish.

½ cup sea salt

½ cup granulated sugar

1½ teaspoons freshly ground black pepper

1½ teaspoons freshly ground white pepper

1 5-pound skin-on steelhead trout filet, trimmed of belly meat, squared and pin bones removed

¼ cup aquavit

½ cup finely chopped dill

Cucumber Salad

Dill Crème Fra che (see note)

Combine the salt, sugar and peppers in a small bowl. Sprinkle some of the dry spice mix in the bottom of a shallow pan. Rub the flesh of the trout filet with the remaining spice mix. Place the filet, skin side down, in the pan. Drizzle with the aquavit and coat with the dill.

Cover with plastic wrap, pressing down tightly over and around the fish. Place another pan on top, and weight it with a heavy object. Refrigerate for 4 days. Flip the fish, and refrigerate for 4 more days. Remove the fish from the pan. Wrap the filet in plastic and refrigerate until needed. It will keep for one month refrigerated and up to six months frozen.

To serve, top thin slices of the gravlax with a dollop of the dill crème fraiche. Accompany with cucumber salad and rye crackers or brown bread.

Note: To make Dill Crème Fraîche, combine 1 cup crème fraiche, 1/2 tablespoon chopped fresh dill and 1/4 teaspoon each sea salt and freshly ground black pepper.

## CUCUMBER SALAD

MAKES ABOUT 2 CUPS

Seedless cucumbers are best for this salad.

| | |
|---|---|
| 1 pound cucumbers, thinly sliced | 1/4 teaspoon fine sea salt |
| 1/2 cup thinly sliced red onions | 1/8 teaspoon freshly ground black pepper |
| 1/4 cup grapeseed oil | |
| 2 tablespons champagne vinegar | 1 tablespoon fresh dill, finely chopped |

In a large bowl, combine the cucumbers, onions, oil, vinegar, salt, pepper and dill. Toss to mix well. Allow to sit for 20 minutes before serving.

# MINT CURED RAINBOW TROUT
## WITH FOUR-PARSLEY SAUCE

I admit to a bit of poetic license with the name of this recipe, inspired by the trio of tender green herbs that go into the sauce along with coriander seeds, which produce cilantro when planted. Their flavors nicely complement the fresh mint used in the cure. You'll probably have sauce left over; it keeps well in the refrigerator for a week.

**FOR THE FISH**

6 boneless, skin-on rainbow trout filets (about 2 1/4 pounds), bellies trimmed and pin bones removed

1/4 cup sea salt

1/4 cup sugar

3/4 cup freshly ground black pepper

1/2 cup mint

2 tablespoons cognac or brandy

2 tablespoons dry white wine

**FOR THE SAUCE**

2 egg yolks

1/2 teaspoon sea salt

1/2 teaspoon freshly ground white pepper

1/4 cup minced garlic

3 cups grapeseed oil

1 tablespoon fresh lemon juice

1/2 teaspoon Dijon mustard

1 tablespoon flat-leaf parsley, chopped

1 tablespoon cilantro, chopped

1 tablespoon chervil, chopped

1 teaspoon toasted, ground coriander seed

For the trout: Combine the salt, sugar and pepper in a small bowl. Rub the spice mix over the flesh of the fish. Distribute half the mint on the bottom of a baking dish. Place 3 trout filets on the mint, skin side down. Drizzle the fish with the cognac and brandy, and top it with remaining mint. Place the remaining trout filets, skin side up, on top of the fish in the baking dish. Cover with plastic wrap, pressing down tightly over and around the fish. Place another pan on top, and weight it with a heavy object.

Refrigerate for 2 days. Pour off any liquid from the bottom of the baking dish, and discard the plastic wrap. Flip the fish, and cover with fresh plastic wrap. Replace the weight, and return the fish to the refrigerator for 2 more days.

For the sauce: Blend the egg yolks with the salt, pepper and garlic in a food processor on high speed. With the motor running, slowly add the oil in a thin stream until well emulsified. Blend in the lemon juice and mustard. Transfer to a medium bowl. Fold in the parsley, cilantro, chervil and coriander seed.

To serve, slice the fish thinly on the diagonal and enjoy with some of the sauce.

# FENNEL-CURED WHITEFISH
## WITH DANISH BROWN BREAD SALAD

This recipe employs our native whitefish, drawing inspiration from a classic Danish dish. Similar to gravlax in method but not in flavor, it is traditionally accompanied by a brown bread salad and served during the winter holiday season when fresh fish is difficult to come by. Note that it takes 4 days to cure the fish.

**FOR THE WHITEFISH**

1 cup grapeseed oil

1/2 cup fennel fronds, finely chopped

1/2 cup sea salt

1/2 cup sugar

1 teaspoon freshly ground black pepper

1 teaspoon freshly ground fennel seeds

2 1/4 pound boneless skin-on whitefish filets, trimmed of belly meat and squared with a sharp knife

1 tablespoon chopped fresh dill

**FOR THE BROWN BREAD SALAD**

1 cup oven dried brown bread cubes (such as pumpernickel)

1/4 cup seeded, chopped tomatoes

1/2 cup very thinly sliced sweet onion

2 tablespoons grapeseed oil

For the whitefish: In a small bowl, make a paste by combining the oil, fennel fronds, salt, sugar, pepper and fennel seeds. Coat the whitefish filets with the paste. Place one filet skin side down in a roasting pan or baking dish. Place the other filet skin side up on top. Cover with plastic wrap, taking care to press it down tightly over and around the fish. Place another pan on top, and weight it with a heavy object. Refrigerate for two days.

Uncover the pan, flip the fish, rewrap and refrigerate for two more days. Remove the fish from the pan and scrape off the fennel paste. Discard the paste and any accumulated juices. Pat the fish dry, and coat it with freshly chopped dill. Wrap the filets individually, and refrigerate or freeze until needed.

To make the salad, combine the bread, tomato, onion and oil in a medium bowl and toss well. Using a very sharp knife, slice the whitefish very thinly by cutting only so far as the skin on a radical bias beginning with the tail and moving toward the head. Make sure to leave the skin on your cutting board. Arrange the sliced fish on chilled serving plates. Add some of the bread salad to each plate and serve immediately.

# TURKEY RILLETTES
## WITH HONEYCRISP APPLE MUSTARD

SERVES 6

We make this recipe with turkey leg confit, prepared exactly the same way as the Duck Confit recipe on page 201. Duck confit makes an equally delicious option.

2 1/2 pound shredded turkey leg confit

1/4 cup chopped garlic

I tablespoon fresh thyme

2 tablespoons Madeira or brandy

2 cups rendered pork or duck fat

Honeycrisp Apple Mustard (page 253)

Thinly sliced raisin bread, toasted

Combine the shredded turkey confit, garlic and thyme in a large nonreactive saucepan. Add the Madeira and 1 cup of the fat. Heat until the fat is completely liquefied and the Madeira is fully absorbed. Divide the mixture among several small crocks, filling them one quarter inch short of completely full.

Meanwhile, liquefy the remaining fat in the same saucepan. Carefully pour the fat into each crock to seal the meat and refrigerate. Serve with the mustard and raisin toast.

# MIDWESTERN COUNTRY PÂTÉ

At Heartland, we buy whole animals from local farms. This allows our farmers to earn more profits, but on our end, it necessitates finding practical uses for every part of the animal, tail through head. This very hearty terrine is our take on the French classic pâté de campagne using lesser cuts of pork and veal. It benefits from the balance provided by a piquant chutney, a fruity mustard and some baby greens tossed in a little verjus—the pressed juice of unripened grapes. We use microgreens from DragSmith Farm in Barron, Wisconsin, and our verjus comes from local vineyards.

I substitute verjus for vinegar and oil when dressing the greens because the chutney and mustard provide enough acidity to offset the terrine's richness. Also, the greens are so delicate that oil tends to weigh them down, which defeats the brightness they bring to the plate. Delicate baby lettuces or very young arugula are fine substitutes for the microgreens.

| | |
|---|---|
| 1 large sweet onion, finely diced | 1/2 teaspoon ground nutmeg |
| 1 teaspoon unsalted butter | 1/2 teaspoon ground allspice |
| 2 pounds ground wild boar or pork shoulder | 1/4 teaspoon ground ginger |
| 1/2 pound ground veal shoulder | 1/4 teaspoon ground mace |
| 1/2 pound diced lean pork | 1/4 teaspoon juniper berries, freshly ground |
| 2 ounces hazelnuts, toasted | 3/4 cup brandy |
| 1 teaspoon thyme leaves | 2 eggs, lightly beaten |
| 1 teaspoon chopped Italian parsley | 1/4 cup all-purpose flour, sifted |
| 1 1/2 teaspoons sea salt | 1 pound slab bacon, sliced extra thin |
| 1/2 teaspoon freshly ground black pepper | 1 Pickled Calves' Tongue (page 54), optional |

In a small skillet, sweat the onions in the butter over moderately low heat until tender. In a large nonreactive bowl, mix the ground boar, veal, pork, hazelnuts, thyme, parsley, salt, pepper, nutmeg, allspice, ginger, mace, juniper berries and brandy until well blended. Allow onions to cool to room temperature and incorporate into meat mixture. Cover mixture with plastic wrap, pressing down firmly so no air can come into contact with it. Refrigerate overnight.

*(recipe continues)*

Preheat the oven to 350°F. In a small bowl, beat the eggs and flour into a fine paste. Add to the meat mixture and mix well. Line a bread pan with the bacon, completely covering the bottom and sides and ensuring there is excess bacon to fold over the top of the pâté. Place half the meat mixture in the bottom of the pan and pack firmly.

If using the tongue, press it firmly into the meat. Add the remaining meat mixture, packing it evenly. Fold the excess bacon over top, tucking into the sides of the terrine. Bang the pan on the counter and press with your hands to eliminate any air pockets.

Place the bread pan in a larger pan or baking dish filled halfway with water and place in the oven. Check the pâté temperature after 45 minutes and continue to check every 15 minutes until the internal temperature reaches 140°F. Remove from the oven, discard the water bath and place pate on a sheet pan. Press firmly with another bread pan of equal size, being mindful of any hot grease that may escape. Place a heavy weight or object inside the top pan. Refrigerate overnight to set.

To remove the pâté from the pan, run a knife around the edge, turn upside down and tap firmly on bottom of the pan until it releases. Serve immediately or wrap in plastic and refrigerate for up to two weeks.

To serve, center a slice of pate on a small plate. Place 1 tablespoon each Cranberry-Apple Chutney (page 257) and Honeycrisp Apple Mustard (page 253) alongside. Garnish with lightly dressed microgreens.

## THE POWER OF A WELL-PICKLED TONGUE

A few years ago, I was meeting with Thomasin Franken, daughter of U.S. Senator Al Franken of Minnesota. Thomasin started out as a third-grade teacher in the Bronx before graduating from the French Culinary Institute. Then she became Director of Extended Learning for DC Prep, a charter school in Washington, D.C. At the time, I was working with several youth- and community-focused initiatives on nutrition, food literacy and broadening access to healthful whole foods for the economically disenfranchised.

It was Labor Day and Heartland was closed, so Thomasin and I sat in the lounge exchanging information and ideas. She was returning to Washington that afternoon, and we were waiting for Al to pick her up and to take her to the airport. I was in the middle of one of my rants about the negative impact of our current food system on the environment, food safety, public health and the fate of small family farms when Al arrived. As always, he graciously listened to my opinions and offered some feedback on what he saw to be the challenges we face in Washington.

Eventually, I calmed down, and Al saw his opportunity: he asked if I had any pickled beef tongue in the house. I took him and Thomasin downstairs to the restaurant's meat locker. I packed up a tongue and made Thomasin promise to share it with her parents when they got back to D.C. felt so proud. No matter how humble, the power of a well-pickled tongue should not be underestimated.

# PICKLED CALVES' TONGUES

My friends in the Twin Cities' Jewish community, for whom well-prepared tongue is a delicacy not to be undervalued, have given this recipe great reviews. I adapted it years ago from one of Charlie Trotter's recipes for pickled lamb tongue, and it can be used for lamb, veal, beef, bison or pork with equal success. Serve thinly sliced tongue with mustard. It makes a great sandwich with even more mustard and pickles. Note that the tongues must soak for at least 24 hours.

2 calves' tongues (about 1 pound each) trimmed

2 tablespoons rendered duck fat

12 whole allspice

1/4 cup coarsely chopped celery

1/4 cup coarsely chopped carrots

1/4 cup coarsely chopped onions

2 garlic cloves, minced

2 teaspoons ground ginger

2 teaspoons minced shallots

1 cinnamon stick

1 tablespoon sea salt

2 teaspoons freshly ground black pepper

1 cup apple cider vinegar

1 cup brown sugar, packed

1/2 cup Brown Veal Stock (page 269)

Submerge the tongues in a large container of cold water and refrigerate. Soak, changing the water twice, until it remains clear over the course of one day. Pat tongues dry.

Melt the duck fat over moderate heat in a large nonreactive skillet. Add the allspice and toast in the fat for 1 minute. Add the tongues and brown on all sides. Add the celery, carrots and onions. Cook until vegetables are soft, about 5 minutes. Add the garlic, ginger, shallots, cinnamon, salt, pepper, vinegar, sugar and veal stock. Stir to dissolve the sugar and bring to a boil. Cover, reduce heat and simmer until the tongues are tender, about 2 hours.

Remove from the heat and let the tongues cool in pickling solution. When cool enough to handle, remove and carefully peel off outside layer of tough tissue. Place in an airtight container and pour pickling solution over the tongues until submerged. They may be refrigerated for up to 3 weeks. To serve, slice very thinly on the diagonal.

# THE ESSENTIAL BRAUNSCHWEIGER

MAKES 5 1-POUND SAUSAGES

We go through a lot of pigs every year at Heartland. Given the large population of ethnic Germans in our area, I didn't have to think too hard about what to do with the many pounds of pork liver we end up with.

Braunschweiger is so popular in Minnesota that almost every farm family of German descent has their own recipe. I've combined a few heirloom recipes with my own interpretation of this classic liver sausage. It makes a great sandwich on pumpernickel bread with sliced raw sweet onions and spicy mustard.

Braunschweiger is essentially a pâté that is usually shaped into a sausage, and the flavor will improve with a day or two of aging. It is often lightly smoked after cooking, so if you have access to a smoker, this can be done over low heat for about 20 minutes, and it vastly improves the flavor. To prepare the pork liver, cook at a low boil in a large saucepan of water for about 20 minutes. Drain, cool, chop coarsely and grind in a meat grinder or pulse to grind in a food processor.

2 1/2 pounds boiled ground pork liver

2 1/2 pounds ground pork

1 cup grated onion

1 tablespoon sugar

2 tablespoons sea salt

1 1/2 tablespoons ground mustard powder

2 teaspoons freshly ground white pepper

1/2 teaspoon ground nutmeg

1/4 teaspoon ground allspice

1/2 teaspoon ground ginger

1/2 teaspoon ground cloves

1 tablespoon finely chopped sage

1 tablespoon finely chopped marjoram

Fresh beef or pork sausage casings

In a large nonreactive bowl, combine the liver, pork, onions, sugar, salt, mustard powder, pepper, nutmeg, allspice, ginger, cloves, sage and marjoram. Mix well and cover tightly with plastic wrap. Refrigerate for 1 hour.

Soak the sausage casings in a bowl of cold water. Using a sausage stuffer according to manufacturer's instructions, stuff the casing with the meat mixture at a ratio of 1 sausage to 1 pound. Tie the sausages with kitchen twine in 8- to 12-inch lengths, leaving about 2 inches at the end of each length since the sausage will expand when cooked.

Bring a large pot of salted water to a boil and add the links. Reduce the heat and simmer for about 45 minutes, until they reach an internal temperature of 160°F. Remove from the water and immediately transfer them to an ice bath to chill. At this point the sausages may be sliced and served, or frozen for up to 6 months. Enjoy them with crusty bread and slices of your favorite apple. A hearty dark beer wouldn't hurt either.

## THE PIG MAKES THE CUT

I like to say that we in Minnesota and the upper Midwest are living in "Pig Central." The quality and variety of pigs raised here is on par with or better than what the rest of the world has to offer.

A few years ago when Mega and I were in New York for the first of my James Beard Award nominations for Best Chef Midwest, I visited Cesare Casella of Salumeria Rosi Parmacotto on the Upper East Side. I was excited to meet him and ask him about his extensive house-crafted charcuterie. I was looking for advice since we were just beginning to cure our first prosciutto hams. I was surprised to hear that chef Casella was not making his own prosciutto, but importing it from Italy because he couldn't find domestic pork of high enough quality to satisfy his standards. I told him that I had just contracted with a local farmer to raise Mangalitsa breed pastured pigs fed on grass and acorns and finished on barley. Three years later, those hams were finally ready, and I was not disappointed. Neither was Lidia Bastianich, who came to Heartland and praised them. It's clear that Minnesota farmers are capable of raising pigs that have what it takes to produce world-class charcuterie.

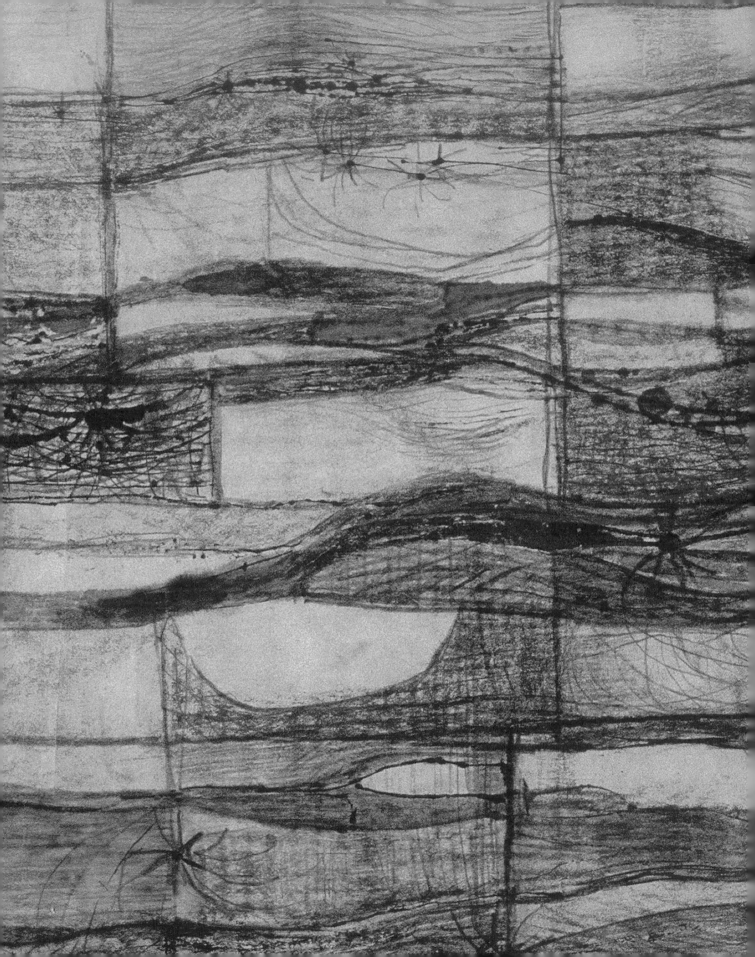

# HOT *and* COLD SOUPS

We cook entirely from scratch utilizing
only whole foods. But sustainability
is as much about the people
who live here as it is about the food.

# HOT *and* COLD SOUPS

---

**TURNIP AND WATERCRESS PUREE**
with Minnesota Crayfish • 61

**GREEN GAZPACHO** • 62

**CHILLED SUMMER MELON SOUP** • 64

**HEIRLOOM TOMATO CREAM SOUP** • 65

**TRICOLOR UKRAINIAN BORSCHT**
with Dill Crème Fraiche • 67

**PINTO BEAN, SPINACH AND PRESERVED
TOMATO SOUP** • 69

**WHITE LENTIL SOUP**
with Red Pepper Coulis • 72

**GREEN ASPARAGUS SOUP**
with Celery Seed Sour Cream and Toasted Hazelnuts • 74

# TURNIP AND WATERCRESS PUREE
## WITH MINNESOTA CRAYFISH

SERVES 6 TO 8

In Scandinavia, root vegetables are called root fruits. That speaks to how well regarded turnips, rutabagas, carrots, celeriac and parsley root are in colder countries, and so it goes in Minnesota. At Heartland, we love the turnip and use it in all shapes, sizes and colors. For this soup, I leave the choice up to you. Keep in mind that the classic purple top turnip is the spiciest, the golden turnip creamiest and the scarlet turnip sweetest.

Red bell peppers add a little sweetness while providing a nice jolt of color, but they're simply members of the supporting cast. The true star is the turnip.

I teaspoon unsalted butter

2 pounds turnips, peeled and diced

¼ pound carrots, peeled and diced

I leek (white part only), chopped

I small shallot, sliced

I large garlic clove, smashed

2 ribs celery, diced

2 large red bell peppers, cored, seeded and diced

I small bay leaf

½ cup dry white wine

I quart Crayfish Stock (page 272) or fish stock

I bunch watercress, stemmed

2 cups heavy cream

2 teaspoons sea salt

I teaspoon freshly ground white pepper

¼ teaspoon cayenne pepper

½ teaspoon ground nutmeg

2 tablespoons cream sherry

½ pound crayfish tail meat, cooked

Watercress sprigs, trimmed, for garnish

Melt the butter in a large soup pot over moderate heat and add the turnips, carrots, leeks, shallot, garlic, celery, bell peppers and bay leaf. Sweat until tender but not browned, about 5 minutes. Add the white wine and deglaze the pan, stirring and scraping the bottom with a wooden spoon. Discard the bay leaf and add the crayfish stock. Bring to a boil, then reduce heat and simmer for 30 minutes.

Remove from the heat and stir in the watercress. Working in batches, purée the soup in a blender while slowly incorporating the cream. Add the salt, peppers, nutmeg and sherry. Blend well.

To serve, add the crayfish to the warm soup. Allow it to rest for 2 minutes, or until the crayfish is warmed through. Garnish each bowl with sprigs of watercress.

# GREEN GAZPACHO

In this riff on traditional gazpacho, we use a variety of late summer green fruits and vegetables at peak ripeness. It's remarkably easy to prepare once the ingredients have been assembled, and is perfect with a glass of dry rosé or crisp Riesling.

I have found that adding sweet red wine vinegar, such as Banyuls, not only brightens the soup but also gives it a cheery, not-too-sweet note that you just don't get from standard red wine vinegar. The chive sour cream garnish accentuates the puréed onions, countering the natural acidity produced by the fruit and vinegar.

I cup peeled, seeded and roughly chopped honeydew melon

I tablespoon seeded, chopped jalapeño

1/4 cup seeded, chopped green bell pepper

1/4 cup chopped green onions

I cup diced white onions

1/2 cup chopped seedless, unpeeled cucumbers

I cup husked and chopped tomatillos

2 tablespoons chopped Italian parsley

2 tablespoons Banyuls vinegar or other red wine vinegar

I teaspoon fine sea salt

1/2 teaspoon freshly ground white pepper

Chive Sour Cream

In a blender, combine the melon, jalapeños, peppers, green and white onions, cucumbers, tomatillos, parsley, vinegar, salt and pepper and puree until smooth. Refrigerate until ready to serve. Garnish each serving with a dollop of Chive Sour Cream.

## CHIVE SOUR CREAM

This is grand on a baked potato, of course, and makes a lush garnish for almost any cold soup when fresh chives are in season.

I cup sour cream

2 tablespoons chopped chives

I teaspoon sea salt

1/2 teaspoon freshly ground black pepper

In a medium bowl, combine the sour cream, chives, salt and pepper. Whisk to blend well and refrigerate until ready to use.

# CHILLED SUMMER MELON SOUP

SERVES 6

This easy summertime favorite works well with many varieties of melons. Feel free to use what's available from your local farm market, and to combine different melons. While appealing as a first course, this soup is also appropriate as a main course for lunch with a salad of garden greens dressed in a sweeter style vinaigrette, or even as an interesting alternative to dessert. For the Raspberry Crème Fraiche, simply add ¼ cup pureed raspberries to 1 cup crème fraiche.

I quart peeled, seeded and coarsely chopped ripe melon (honeydew, musk or Juan Canary)

½ cup sweet white wine such as Riesling or muscat

¼ cup chopped mint

I teaspoon ground cinnamon

½ teaspoon ground ginger

¼ teaspoon ground nutmeg

¼ teaspoon ground allspice

¼ cup honey

6 tablespoons Raspberry Crème Fra che

30 fresh raspberries

Purée the melon, wine, mint, cinnamon, ginger, nutmeg, allspice and honey in a blender until smooth. Refrigerate until ready to serve.

To serve, divide the soup among chilled bowls. Garnish each serving with a tablespoon of Raspberry Crème Fraîche and 5 fresh raspberries.

## CRÈME FRAÎCHE

MAKES ABOUT 5½ CUPS

I quart heavy cream

1½ cups buttermilk

In a large nonreactive bowl, combine the cream and buttermilk. Cover with cheesecloth and allow it to stand at room temperature for 72 hours, or until the desired thickness is achieved. Transfer to a container, cover tightly and refrigerate for up to 2 weeks.

# HEIRLOOM TOMATO CREAM SOUP

We make this delectable soup when the heirloom tomatoes are a tad overripe. To skin the tomatoes, cut out the cores and score the bottoms with an "x" before plunging them into boiling water for a few seconds. Transfer immediately to an ice water bath. The skins should slip off. I seed the tomatoes by slicing them crosswise and using my fingers like a citrus reamer. Remove as many as you can, but if a few are missed, it's no big deal.

The garnish is a simple drizzle of sweet vinegar. We ferment our own ice wine vinegar from verjus we get from Alexis Bailly Vineyards in Hastings, Minnesota. Nan Bailly leaves several rows of late harvest grapes on the vine for us until they freeze. This concentrates the sugars, and then she sends us the unfermented grape juice. You can substitute a highly concentrated sweet grape must vinegar, such as uva cotta or mosto d'uva.

2 tablespoons butter

1 1/2 to 2 pounds heirloom tomatoes, seeded and peeled, to yield 1 quart pulp

1 teaspoon paprika

1/2 teaspoon cayenne pepper

2 tablespoons chopped fresh tarragon

2 tablespoons chopped Italian parsley

1 quart heavy cream

2 cups Court-Bouillon (page 268) or vegetable stock

2 tablespoons ice wine vinegar, aged balsamic vinegar or uva cotta

Melt the butter in a large nonreactive pot over moderate heat. Add the tomatoes, paprika and cayenne pepper and simmer for 3 minutes. Add the tarragon and parsley. Simmer for 2 more minutes. Remove from the heat and purée in a blender or food processor.

Return the soup to the pot and heat just to simmering. When the tomato mixture is warm, slowly incorporate the cream and court-bouillon using a wire whisk or wooden spoon. Divide the soup among serving bowls and drizzle with the vinegar. Serve immediately.

# TRICOLOR UKRAINIAN BORSCHT
## WITH DILL CRÈME FRAICHE

The Twin Cities are home to a sizable Ukrainian community. Their devotion to family and to the preservation of their language and culture has always held a special attraction. On Hennepin Avenue in the northeast Minneapolis neighborhood where they first settled, there's a famous Eastern European deli and restaurant called Kramarczuk's, founded by war refugees in 1954. It remains a mecca for sausage lovers to this day, and was a James Beard Award America's Classic honoree in 2013.

I was introduced to Ukrainian borscht 20 years ago in a church kitchen. It was a rustic stew with chunks of beets, cabbage and beef floating in delectable broth topped with sour cream. This version was inspired by those humble origins. I simply refined it for those who tend not to dine at church suppers. (They don't know what they're missing!) Of course you can make this with beets of just one color, but it's fun to pull out all the stops and prepare the whole trio.

**FOR THE RED BORSCHT**

¼ cup grapeseed oil

¼ cup peeled and diced carrots

¼ cup diced onions

¼ cup diced celery

2 small garlic cloves, peeled and crushed

1 shallot, peeled and sliced

1 pound red beets, roasted, peeled and diced

¼ cup dry red wine

1 cup Chicken Stock (page 267)

1 tablespoon chopped Italian parsley

1 teaspoon sea salt

½ teaspoon freshly ground white pepper

1 cup Dill Crème Fraiche

Gold Borscht

Green Borscht

To prepare the red borscht, heat the oil in a large nonreactive pot over moderately low heat. Add the carrots, onions, celery, garlic and shallot and sweat until tender, about 5 minutes. Add the beets, wine and stock. Increase the heat and simmer, covered, for 30 minutes. Transfer to a blender, working in batches if necessary, and purée until smooth. Season with the salt and pepper.

For the gold borscht, follow the instructions for red borscht in the same quantities, substituting gold beets for the red, white wine for the red wine and ½ teaspoon freshly ground nutmeg for the parsley.

*(recipe continues)*

To serve, reheat the red and gold borschts in separate pans if necessary. The green borscht is served uncooked. It's important that you work with confidence when plating the tricolor borscht. Using two 4-ounce ladles, simultaneously pour 1 ladle of red borscht and 1 ladle of gold borscht into opposite sides of the same heated shallow soup dish. This takes a little practice, but don't be intimidated. If done correctly, the bowl will have roughly two equal sides of red and gold borscht. Swirl 1 ounce of the green borscht over the top, then swirl in the crème fraîche. Serve immediately.

## GREEN BORSCHT

MAKES ABOUT 3 CUPS

This light, nourishing uncooked soup tastes great on its own or as part of the showier tricolor borscht presentation. The recipe makes a fine vegan meal without the crème fraîche. If you can't find the springtime perennial herb sorrel, substitute more spinach.

| | |
|---|---|
| 1/2 pound sorrel, stemmed | 1 tablespoon freshly squeezed lemon juice |
| 1/2 pound spinach, stemmed | 1/2 cup cold Court-Bouillon (page 268) |
| 1 small sweet onion, peeled and chopped | 1 teaspoon sea salt |
| 4 ounces basil leaves | 1/2 teaspoon freshly ground white pepper |

In a food processor, combine the sorrel, spinach, onions, basil, lemon juice, court-bouillon, salt and pepper. Pulse to a fine purée; a slightly coarse texture is also good. Refrigerate until needed.

## DILL CRÈME FRAÎCHE

| | |
|---|---|
| 1 cup Crème Fra che (page 64) | 1 teaspoon sea salt |
| 2 tablespoons chopped fresh dill | 1/2 teaspoon freshly ground black pepper |

In a stainless steel bowl, combine the crème fraiche, dill, salt and pepper. Stir with a spoon to mix well, cover and refrigerate until ready to use.

# PINTO BEAN, SPINACH AND PRESERVED TOMATO SOUP

This early winter soup features spinach from our greenhouse growers. We rely on greenhouse and hydroponic suppliers for fresh greens as we head out of the short Minnesota growing season. The soup also uses our local storage crop of onions, garlic and dried beans as well as preserved tomatoes from the larder. When cooking the beans, don't salt the water as the beans will get tough and take longer to cook. This makes a lot of soup, so be sure to freeze some for next time.

2 pounds dried pinto beans

I onion, peeled and studded with 3 cloves

2 large carrots, peeled

I bay leaf

I quart Chicken Stock (page 267)

6 cups spinach leaves

I cup sliced preserved or sundried tomatoes

2 garlic cloves, sliced

I teaspoon sea salt

1/2 teaspoon freshly ground black pepper

2 tablespoons chopped oregano

Grated Parmesan serving (optional)

In a large, nonreactive pot, soak the beans in cold water to cover for about 8 hours at room temperature.

Drain and rinse the beans. Return the beans to the pot and add the onion, carrots and bay leaf. Cover with fresh water. Bring to a boil, then reduce to a simmer. Cook until the beans are tender, about 1 hour.

Drain the beans and reserve the cooking liquid. Discard the onion, carrot and bay leaf. Return the cooked beans to the pot along with the cooking liquid and chicken stock. Bring to a simmer over moderate heat. Add the spinach, tomatoes and garlic. Simmer for 5 minutes. Season with the salt and pepper, and stir in the oregano. Garnish each serving with freshly grated Parmesan cheese if you like.

# WHITE LENTIL SOUP
## WITH RED PEPPER COULIS

SERVES 12

Earthy and flavorful, this soup enhanced with roasted garlic is equally appealing in summer or winter. It showcases the unusual white lentil cultivar grown throughout the Midwest. More delicately flavored than the common green or black varieties, white lentils lend themselves well to warm-weather dishes. Red Pepper Coulis provides a bright counterpoint to the creamy bean soup.

2 pounds split white lentils, rinsed and checked for stones

I onion, peeled and studded with 3 cloves

I large carrot, peeled

Bouquet garni (2 parsley sprigs, 2 thyme sprigs, I bay leaves, 2 garlic cloves, 10 black peppercorns)

2 quarts Court-Bouillon (page 268) or vegetable stock

2 cups reserved lentil cooking liquid

2 heads roasted garlic, peeled and purée

1/4 cup Madeira

1 1/2 tablespoons sea salt

3/4 tablespoon freshly ground white pepper

Red Pepper Coulis

Chopped parsley or chives for garnish

To prepare the lentils, combine in a large pot with 2 quarts of cold water, onion, carrot and bouquet garni. Bring to a boil, reduce to a simmer and gently cook until the lentils are soft, about 1 hour. Drain the lentils, reserving the cooking liquid. Remove the onion, carrot and bouquet garni. Purée the lentils in a blender or food processor until smooth.

To prepare the soup, combine the puréed lentils, court-bouillon, reserved cooking liquid, garlic, Madeira, salt and pepper in a large pot. Simmer slowly, stirring frequently to avoid sticking, for about 30 minutes.

For each serving, drizzle a tablespoon of the Red Pepper Coulis over the top. Garnish with a little chopped fresh parsley or chives. Serve immediately.

## RED PEPPER COULIS

MAKES ABOUT 2 CUPS

5 pounds red bell peppers,
cored and seeded

2 garlic cloves

1/2 cup diced onions

1 cup white wine

1 cup water

1 teaspoon sea salt

1/2 teaspoon cayenne pepper

1/2 teaspoon paprika

In a large nonreactive pot, combine the peppers, garlic, onions, wine, water, salt, pepper and paprika. Simmer for 20 to 25 minutes, until the vegetables are soft. Remove from the heat.

Purée the vegetables in a blender or food processor until smooth. To attain the perfectly smooth texture of the coulis we serve at Heartland, run the puree through a food mill too. It should be the consistency of catsup. If it's runny, return to the stove and cook gently over low heat until reduced to the desired consistency. Cover and refrigerate.

# GREEN ASPARAGUS SOUP

WITH CELERY SEED SOUR CREAM AND TOASTED HAZELNUTS

SERVES 6

This delicate, mint-scented soup is one of the first recipes we return to when spring arrives in Minnesota each year. I have demonstrated it numerous times at local farmers, markets and in front of a camera for our local television broadcast affiliates. It never fails to draw praise from those who have tried it at home.

2 pounds asparagus, trimmed of woody ends

3 spring onions, trimmed

I cup sour cream

I teaspoon celery seed, lightly toasted

I cup mint leaves

2 cups Court-Bouillon (page 268) or vegetable broth

1/2 teaspoon sea salt

1/4 teaspoon freshly ground white pepper

I cup heavy cream (optional)

1 1/2 teaspoons lightly toasted hazelnuts, papery husks removed and coarsely chopped

2 teaspoons chopped chives

Bring a large pot of salted water to the boil and set up an ice water bath. Plunge the asparagus and spring onions into the boiling water and blanch until tender, about 3 minutes. Drain and transfer to the ice water bath just until chilled. Remove and drain on paper towels.

In a small nonreactive bowl, whisk together the sour cream and celery seed, and season with salt and pepper. Cover and refrigerate.

When the vegetables have drained sufficiently, coarsely chop them into 1-inch pieces and place in a high-speed blender or food processor, working in batches if necessary. Add the mint and court-bouillon and purée until smooth. Season to taste with salt and white pepper.

For a richer version of this soup, slowly add the cream with the blender still running until well incorporated. To serve, divide evenly among serving bowls. Drizzle a little celery seed sour cream on top and garnish with the hazelnuts and chives.

# GRAINS, PASTA
*and*
# BEANS

Wild rice is an American original, like the
bison that once roamed the plains. It is our honor
to source this rice from the White Earth Nation,
the very people who first discovered it.

# GRAINS, PASTA
### *and*
# BEANS

ESCAROLE AND BEANS • 79

SWEET CORN-BLACK BARLEY CAKES • 81

LENTILS WITH SMOKED PORK • 82

WILD RICE AND APPLE RELISH • 83

ROASTED PUMPKIN BARLEY RISOTTO • 86

SHELL PEA BARLEY RISOTTO
with Crisp Leeks • 88

WINTER VEGETABLE FARRO • 89

WILD MUSHROOM FARRO • 91

POLENTA FRIES • 92

GNUDI MARINARA • 97

POTATO GNOCCHI
with Chanterelles, Arugula and Tomato • 99

HAZELNUT RAVIOLI
with Mint Butter • 102

DUCK LIVER RAVIOLI
with Mushrooms and Sage Cream • 105

# ESCAROLE AND BEANS

I ate a lot of escarole and beans when I was growing up in Hoboken. It's a staple of the Italian immigrant kitchen. When we got bored with that, we changed it up and had beans with escarole. It is extremely economical, a balanced and nutritious bowlful that feeds a deep hunger. Don't salt the beans until they're tender, or they may toughen.

2 cups (1 pound) great northern or cannellini beans

1 onion, peeled and studded with cloves

2 large carrots, peeled

1 bay leaf

1/4 cup grapeseed, sunflower or extra virgin olive oil

6 cups escarole, coarsely chopped

2 garlic cloves, minced

1 1/2 cups Chicken Stock (page 267)

1 teaspoon sea salt

1/2 teaspoon freshly ground black pepper

1/4 teaspoon cracked red pepper, optional

1/2 cup grated Parmesan or aged sheep cheese

Soak the beans in a bowl of cold water to cover for 6 to 8 hours at room temperature.

Drain and rinse the beans. Place in a large pot with the onion, carrots and bay leaf, and cover with cold water. Bring to a boil, then reduce the heat to a simmer. Cook until the beans are tender, about 1 hour. Drain the beans, discarding the vegetables and bay leaf.

In a soup pot or dutch oven, warm the oil over moderate heat, add the escarole and saute until tender, 3 to 5 minutes. Add the garlic and cook for 2 minutes. Add the beans and stock. Cover and cook for 3 minutes. Season with salt, pepper and red pepper if using. Just before serving, grate Parmesan on top.

# SWEET CORN-BLACK BARLEY CAKES

These delicious vegetarian patties combine sweet corn and barley, two crops grown in abundance in Minnesota. I really like the contrast of black barley with yellow corn kernels, but regular white barley is fine too. Whichever you choose, be sure to cook it thoroughly; undercooked barley can turn hard when fried. For a decadent appetizer, top the cakes with paddlefish caviar and a dab of sour cream. They're also good with braised spinach and a poached egg, or a ragoût of wild mushrooms. This is a large batch, but they make nourishing leftovers.

2 tablespoons finely chopped onions

3 tablespoons unsalted butter, divided

2 tablespoons finely diced celery

2 tablespoons finely diced carrots

1/4 cup chopped scallions

2 cups cooked black barley

1/3 cup corn kernels, blanched

1 cup all-purpose flour

1/2 cup panko bread crumbs

1 teaspoons sea salt

1/2 teaspoon freshly ground black pepper

2 tablespoons chopped flat-leaf parsley

1 large egg, lightly beaten

In a large skillet, sauté the onions in 1 tablespoon of butter over moderate heat until lightly browned. Add the celery, carrots, scallions, barley and corn. Continue to cook until vegetables and barley are tender, about 5 minutes. Stir in the flour and cook for 1 minute longer. Remove from the heat and cool to room temperature.

In a large bowl, combine the panko, salt, pepper, parsley and egg. Add the barley and mix well. Shape into 12 cakes of equal size, about 1 inch thick.

In a nonstick skillet, heat the remaining 2 tablespoons butter over moderate heat until it begins to foam. Working in batches, fry the cakes on both sides until lightly browned, about 2 minutes per side. Keep warm in a low oven until they've all been fried, then serve immediately.

# LENTILS WITH SMOKED PORK

This is an elemental stew that makes a hearty lunch on a rainy day. Serve it in large bowls with a salad of bitter greens in light vinaigrette. Lentils are drought resistant, which make them a good crop for hot summers with sparse rainfall which we often experience here in the Upper Midwest. Our lentils, which come in various colors, sizes and flavor profiles, are from Chieftain Wild Rice Company in Spooner, Wisconsin. Because they are a pulse, or a grain legume, they lend themselves well to crop rotation since they actively fix nitrogen to the soil during the growing season. Consequently, lentils are one cover crop that can also be harvested for profit by regional farmers.

| | |
|---|---|
| 2 cups (1 pound) lentils, rinsed and checked for stones | Bouquet garni (2 parsley sprigs, 2 thyme sprigs, 1 bay leaf, 2 garlic cloves, 10 black peppercorns) |
| 1 smoked pork hock or ham bone, or 1/4 pound diced smoked bacon | 1 teaspoon sea salt |
| 1 small yellow onion, peeled and studded with 3 -cloves | 1/2 teaspoon freshly ground black pepper |
| 1 medium carrot, peeled | Virgin sunflower oil or extra virgin olive oil, for drizzing |

Combine the lentils in a large pot with 4 cups of cold water. Add the pork hock, onion, carrot and bouquet garni. Bring to a boil, then reduce the heat to a simmer and gently cook until the lentils are tender but still firm, about 30 minutes.

Partially drain the lentils, leaving enough broth to keep them moist. Remove the pork hock, vegetables and bouquet garni. Pull the meat from the pork hock and return it to the lentils. Adjust the seasoning with the salt and pepper. Serve immediately with a drizzle of virgin sunflower oil or extra virgin olive oil.

# WILD RICE AND APPLE RELISH

The simplest recipes are often the most satisfying. This relish is more like a wild rice salad than a condiment, and is a great accompaniment to a grilled pork chop hot off the fire. I prefer Cortland apples here, though any sweet red apple will do. The Cortland, a cross between the McIntosh and the Ben Davis with streaked bright red and golden skin, is a relatively small fruit that was developed in upstate New York but thrives in Minnesota. Its natural sweetness holds up well in a vinegar-based dressing. To keep apples from turning brown, submerge them in a bowl of cold water with a dash of apple cider vinegar as you cut them into small dice.

1 1/2 cups wild rice, rinsed well

3 1/2 cups water

2 teaspoons sea salt, divided

1/4 cup apple cider vinegar

1/2 cup grapeseed oil

1/2 cup chopped tarragon

1/2 teaspoon freshly ground black pepper

3 pounds apples (about 12 Cortland or 10 medium), cored and cut into small dice

In a medium saucepan, combine the wild rice with water and 1 teaspoon salt. Bring to a boil, cover and reduce the heat to a simmer. Cook for 45 minutes, then check to see if the kernels have popped, indicating the grain is tender. If not, continue to cook, checking every 5 minutes. The rice should be tender but not mushy, slightly chewy but not crunchy. It might be necessary to add a bit more water during cooking. Once the rice is done, drain and fluff with a fork.

In a nonreactive bowl, whisk together the apple cider vinegar and remaining salt, then add the oil, tarragon and pepper and whisk to combine. Toss the apples and wild rice with the dressing. It's fine if the wild rice has not fully cooled, because slightly warm rice will better absorb the flavors of the dressing.

# WHITE EARTH WILD RICE

Minnesota's largest Native American nation calls itself Anishinaabe, "the original people." Early settlers called them Ojibwe, probably a derivative of the native word "ojib," a type of puckered moccasin and a word further transformed into "Chippewa." Large numbers of Anishinaabe had settled in northern Minnesota by 1400 A.D., fully 400 years before any Europeans made their way there.

Today, as a result of an 1867 treaty between the United States and the Mississippi Band of Chippewa Indians, the Anishinaabe of the White Earth Nation live in Becker, Walker and Mahnomen counties of northern Minnesota. There they harvest wild rice, the "food that grows on water" known to them as manoomin, a gift from the Great Spirit.

Still harvested by hand in the traditional way with non-motorized canoes, and processed naturally so that it dries a beautiful golden brown, White Earth wild rice is a non-GMO cereal grain gathered from an annual aquatic plant that grows three to eight feet before producing seed pods that extend above the water's surface. These pods are harvested in flat-bed canoes by bending and thrashing the heads to release the ripe kernels. The immature kernels are left to fall back into the water where they will germinate and produce the next year's harvest.

One of only two native North American cereal grains, wild rice is the state grain of Minnesota. White Earth's wild rice is organically certified by the state, and is still cultivated the way it was hundreds of years ago. At Heartland, we make extensive use of both whole grain wild rice and wild rice flour. Low in fat and high in protein, dietary fiber and essential amino acids, its earthy, nutty flavor is the perfect accompaniment to many of our dishes. It can also stand alone as a vegetarian main dish or the backbone of a hearty soup or stew. Unlike many of the imported fruits and vegetables now grown here, wild rice is truly a Minnesota original.

# ROASTED PUMPKIN BARLEY RISOTTO

This risotto is served with our ever-popular Osso Buco (page 167), but it's a surprisingly versatile accompaniment for many meat dishes. And, of course, it makes a superb vegetarian entrée. This recipe yields ample roasted pumpkin for the risotto, with some extra to toss in soup, pasta or a hearty winter salad. Butternut squash is a fine substitute.

**FOR THE ROASTED PUMPKIN**

1 small to medium pie pumpkin, about 3 pounds

1/2 cup grapeseed oil

1/4 teaspoon sea salt

Freshly ground black pepper

Grated nutmeg

**FOR THE RISOTTO**

1 cup Court-Bouillon (page 268) or vegetable broth

1 cup Basic Barley

1 cup roasted pumpkin

2 tablespoons unsalted butter

2 teaspoons chopped tarragon

1/4 cup grated Parmesan cheese

1 teaspoons sea salt

1/2 teaspoon freshly ground black pepper

Preheat the oven to 400°. Halve, seed, peel and dice the pumpkin and toss with the oil, salt, pepper and a dash of grated nutmeg. Place in a single layer on a sheet pan lined with parchment and roast until tender and lightly browned, 20 to 25 minutes. Set aside 1 cup for the risotto and reserve the rest for later use.

In a large saucepan, warm the court-bouillon over moderately low heat. Add the cooked Basic Barley. Stir gently with a wooden spoon until the stock has been completely absorbed, about 2 minutes. Stir in the roasted pumpkin. Add the butter, tarragon and cheese and stir to combine. Season to taste with salt and pepper.

# BASIC BARLEY

MAKES 2 CUPS

At Heartland, we rely on the classic French mixture of sautéed, chopped onion, carrot and celery called mirepoix for adding flavor. When cooking barley, we use a technique called pearlizing, the object of which is to split open the grain so the seasoning reaches the inside of the kernel instead of just the exterior. This recipe produces a partially cooked grain to use in the preceding barley risotto recipe. It's also a great addition to mushroom soup or any hearty vegetable soup.

I quart Court-Bouillon (page 268) or vegetable broth

1/4 cup mirepoix (finely chopped carrots, celery and onion)

1 1/2 teaspoons chopped garlic

I tablespoon grapeseed oil

I cup barley

I teaspoons sea salt

1/4 teaspoon freshly ground black pepper

I tablespoon thyme leaves

In a saucepan, heat the court-bouillon to a simmer. In a large pot, sauté the mirepoix and garlic in the oil over moderate heat until tender but not brown, about 5 minutes. Stir in the barley and toast, stirring occasionally, until it begins to change color, about 5 minutes longer. Season with salt and pepper.

Add 1 cup of the court-bouillon. Stir the barley from the bottom and cook over moderate heat until the liquid is almost completely absorbed. Add the remaining court-bouillon and cook, stirring occasionally, for 20 minutes. Remove from the heat and stir in the thyme.

# SHELL PEA BARLEY RISOTTO
## WITH CRISP LEEKS

Here's an excellent vegetarian dish for spring. I like to serve it beneath a nice piece of fish or pan-roasted chicken. In Minnesota, our season for local fresh peas is so freaking short that we use as many as we can when we get them, and also freeze large quantities of raw peas for the off season. They are one of the few vegetables that will freeze particularly well with no discernible change in quality.

**FOR THE CRISP LEEKS**

2 pounds leeks, thinly sliced

Grapeseed or canola oil, for frying

I tablespoon sea salt

**FOR THE RISOTTO**

2 cups Court-Bouillon (page 268)

2 cups Basic Barley (page 87)

I cup fresh shell peas, blanched

¼ cup unsalted butter

2 teaspoons chopped tarragon

½ cup grated Parmesan

2 teaspoons sea salt

I teaspoon freshly ground black pepper

I cup hot Parmesan Broth (page 9I)

For the crisp leeks: Soak the sliced leeks in cold water for 20 minutes. Drain and pat dry. Heat at least 3 inches of oil to 320°F in a deep fryer or large saucepan with high sides. Carefully add the leeks and fry until crisp, about 1 minute. The leeks will float to the surface when done. Using a slotted spoon, transfer to a sheet pan lined with paper towels. Season with salt. Keep warm or let cool and store in an airtight container.

For the risotto: In a large saucepan, warm the court-bouillon over moderately low heat. Add the cooked Basic Barley. Stir gently with a wooden spoon until the stock has been completely absorbed, about 2 minutes. Stir in the blanched peas. Add the butter, tarragon and cheese, and stir to combine. Season with salt and pepper. Divide among 4 serving bowls, and ladle ¼ cup hot Parmesan Broth around each serving of the risotto. Garnish with the leeks and serve immediately.

# WINTER VEGETABLE FARRO

SERVES 4

This earthy, satisfying side always gets eaten. It's a dish that celebrates the harvest, and I serve variations on it from late autumn until early spring with different seasonal accompaniments. We use greenhouse-grown herbs in winter, and they aren't as assertively flavored as those from the garden. Consequently, to ensure that the tarragon flavor comes through without being overpowered by the walnuts, I use what seems like an awful lot of the herb.

I cup peeled, diced winter squash

I cup peeled, diced root vegetables such as turnip, rutabagas and celeriac

I tablespoon grapeseed oil

Sea salt, to taste

Freshly grated nutmeg

2 cups Court-Bouillon (page 268) or vegetable broth

2 cups Basic Farro (recipe follows)

¹/2 cup toasted walnuts

¹/4 cup unsalted butter

4 teaspoons chopped tarragon

¹/2 cup grated Parmesan

I teaspoon freshly ground black pepper

I cup Parmesan Broth (page 91) or vegetable broth, warmed

Preheat the oven to 400°F. On a sheet pan lined with parchment, toss the squash and root vegetables with the oil, salt, pepper and nutmeg. Spread out into a single layer and roast, stirring once or twice, until tender and lightly browned, 20 to 25 minutes.

In a large pot, warm the court-bouillon over moderately low heat. Add the Basic Farro. Bring to a simmer and cook, stirring gently with a wooden spoon, until the stock is completely absorbed, about 2 minutes. Add the squash, root vegetables and walnuts. Stir in the butter, tarragon and Parmesan. Season with salt and pepper. Serve with a ladleful of hot Parmesan Broth for each portion to create a loose, creamy texture.

*(recipe continues)*

# BASIC FARRO

This produces a partially cooked farro to use in the preceding recipe. It's also a great last-minute addition to almost any hearty vegetable soup.

2 quarts Court-Bouillon (page 268) or vegetable broth

3/4 cup mirepoix (finely chopped carrots, celery and onion)

1 teaspoon minced garlic

2 tablespoons grapeseed oil

2 cups (1 pound) farro, or soft wheat berries

1 teaspoon sea salt

1/2 teaspoon freshly ground black pepper

2 tablespoons thyme leaves

In a large pot, bring the court-bouillon to a simmer. In a large deep skillet, sauté the carrots, celery, onion and garlic in the oil until tender but not browned, about 5 minutes. Add the farro and sauté, stirring with a wooden spoon, until the farro is shiny and begins to change color. Season with salt and pepper.

Add 1 cup of warm court-bouillon to the farro. Stir from the bottom and allow the stock to become almost completely absorbed by it. Repeat until all the broth has been used and the farro has cooked for 20 minutes. Remove from the heat, season with salt and pepper, and stir in the thyme.

# WILD MUSHROOM FARRO

We serve this as a side, but it makes a worthwhile meatless entrée. The heartiness of the farro combines with the meaty mushrooms to create a dish that is robust but not heavy. I sometimes serve it instead of potatoes with braised rabbit or grilled pork chops.

4 tablespoon unsalted butter, divided

1 pound wild mushrooms, trimmed and cleaned

6 cups Court-Bouillon (page 268)

4 cups Basic Farro

1/2 cup grated Parmesan

1 teaspoon thyme leaves

2 teaspoons sea salt

2 teaspoons freshly ground black pepper

6 cups Parmesan Broth (page 90)

Melt 1 tablespoon butter in a medium skillet over moderate heat and add the mushrooms. Sauté for about 5 minutes, until tender.

In a large saucepan, warm the court-bouillon over moderately low heat. Add the Basic Farro. Bring to a simmer and cook, stirring gently with a wooden spoon, until the stock is completely absorbed, about 2 minutes. Add the mushrooms. Stir in the remaining butter, Parmesan and thyme. Season with salt and pepper. Serve with a ladleful of hot Parmesan Broth for each portion to create a loose, creamy texture.

## PARMESAN BROTH

MAKES 1 QUART

This might be the easiest recipe you ever prepare. Aside from the court-bouillon, there really isn't much to this, but it's a great way to get the most mileage out of leftover Parmesan rinds or cheese that is over aged and too hard to grate. It doesn't require any embellishment since the cheese does all the work for you.

1 quart Court-Bouillon (page 268)

1/2 pound Parmesan rinds

Bring the court-bouillon to a boil in a nonreactive saucepan. Add the cheese rinds. Reduce the heat, and simmer for 20 minutes.

Strain the broth through a fine-mesh sieve lined with dampened cheesecloth. Transfer to containers, cover and refrigerate.

# POLENTA FRIES

I developed this simple recipe while consulting for the restaurants at the Guthrie Theater, because I refused to make French fries. As it turned out, people couldn't get enough of them. Polenta fries became one of those menu monsters that could not be stopped. At one point, I had to assign a cook exclusively to the task of prepping them.

Grapeseed oil or canola oil for frying

I pound cooled, cooked Basic Polenta, cut into 4-inch by 1/2 -inch sticks

2 teaspoons sea salt

Heat at least 3 inches of oil to 320°F in a deep fryer or large saucepan with high sides. Working in batches, carefully add the polenta sticks and fry until crisp, 8 to 10 minutes. They will float to the surface of the oil when done.

Using a slotted spoon, transfer the fries to drain on a sheet pan lined with paper towels. Season while hot with the sea salt. Keep warm or serve immediately.

## BASIC POLENTA

SERVES 6 TO 8

We grow a lot of corn in Minnesota, and we have very high-quality cornmeal, some of which is superb for making polenta. Be prepared for a bit of a workout when you make this, as stirring polenta requires elbow grease. The basic recipe can be prepared ahead, cooled and cut into cakes for grilling or sticks for fries. They keep for at least a week if wrapped well and refrigerated. Try adding a handful of grated sharp Cheddar with the butter and Parmesan.

I tablespoon grapeseed oil or olive oil

3/4 cup mirepoix (finely chopped carrots, celery and onion)

I tablespoon fine sea salt

1 1/2 teaspoons freshly ground black pepper

4 cups fine cornmeal

1/2 pound unsalted butter, cubed

3 cups grated Parmesan

Heat the oil in a medium skillet over moderately low heat. Add the carrots, celery and onion. Saute until tender but not brown, about 5 minutes. Season with the salt and pepper.

Bring 2 quarts of salted water to the boil in a large heavy pot. Slowly add the cornmeal in a thin stream while stirring constantly with a wooden spoon. Reduce the heat to moderate and cook for 25 to 30 minutes, stirring frequently. Remove from the heat and add the vegetables. Stir in the butter and Parmesan. Spread the polenta evenly on sheet pans to cool. Let cool and cut into cakes or sticks as for Polenta Fries.

## LOCAL MILLS

Minnesota is central to America's history of grain and flour production. In fact, Minneapolis earned the nickname "Mill City" because it was once the flour milling capital of the world. In 1860, the city's population was 13,000. Just 20 years later, it had grown to 165,000, thanks in part to advances in technology pioneered by companies like Pillsbury and Washburn-Crosby (later General Mills), which became the leading producers of high-quality flour.

Today, grain and milling industries continue to be mainstays of the Minnesota economy and are important in many other facets of food production and food service. At Heartland, we go to great lengths to source grains, beans and flour from agriculturally sustainable sources, free of genetic modification.

# SHEPHERD'S WAY FARM

---

Fresh sheep's milk ricotta, a veined cheese called Big Woods Blue and Morcella, studded with local morel mushrooms, are among the standout varieties produced at Shepherd's Way Farm, a sheep milk dairy established in 1994 in Nerstrand, rural Carver County, Minnesota. Owners Steven Read and Jodi Ohlsen Read began with an asiago-style cheese called Friesago, and kept increasing their dairy flock until it was one of the largest in North America, with more than 500 sheep and lambs. In 2002, they won their first American Cheese Society Award.

Word spread quickly about the Reads' commitment to quality, animal welfare and sustainable grazing practices, and they were chosen to represent Minnesota and the United States at the first Slow Foods International Terre Madre Conference in Turin, Italy in 2004.

Soon after, a devastating arson fire destroyed the barns and took the lives of most of their flock. It wasn't until 2011, with enormous community support, that Shepherd's Way Farms was able to rebuild and resume full production. The Reads became a symbol of perseverance for everyone associated with farming in Minnesota.

Today, with a much smaller flock of 200 milking ewes, Steven and Jodi have diversified into heritage breed chicken and pigs. Their farm is once again a fixture in local farmers' markets and specialty cheese shops nationwide, and their sons are now firmly entrenched in the farm family way of life as the next generation of shepherds and cheese makers.

# GNUDI MARINARA

Gnudi are essentially stuffed pasta without the pasta—delicate little cheese dumplings bound lightly with flour. Their name comes from *nudo*, the Italian word for naked. I strongly caution against substituting all-purpose flour for the finely ground 00 flour specified. I have tried using all-purpose flour and ended up with heavy dumplings. Gnudi should be light and pillowy morsels that dance on your tongue, not lumps that sit in your stomach. They may be made ahead of time and stored in the freezer.

2 pounds fresh ricotta, preferably sheeps' milk

2 large eggs

2 1/2 ounces pecorino romano, grated

2 teaspoons sea salt

1/2 teaspoon freshly ground white pepper

1 1/2 cups 00 flour, sifted, plus additional flour for tossing

Marinara Sauce

Freshly grated Parmesan

To make the gnudi, line a large fine mesh sieve with dampened cheesecloth. Fill with the ricotta and drain for 1 hour.

In a large bowl, beat the eggs with the pecorino, salt and pepper. Stir in the ricotta. Gradually add the flour while stirring. Do not overwork the dough or the gnudi will be tough. Cover the dough with a towel and let it rest for 1 hour.

Place some additional flour in a large bowl. Divide the gnudi dough in half. Working with one half at a time, roll the dough in the flour until lightly coated. Gently roll the dough into a log about 1/2 inch in diameter. Cut the log into 1-inch pieces. Repeat with the remaining dough.

To cook, bring a large pot of salted water to a boil. Add the gnudi and stir gently. They cook quickly: when they float to the surface, they're done. Gnudi are fragile, so use a slotted spoon or spider strainer to carefully remove them from the boiling water. Transfer immediately to the sauce, and serve right away. They are best when steaming hot. Shave a little fresh parmesan cheese over top. Buon appetito!

*(recipe continues)*

# MARINARA SAUCE

MAKES ABOUT 2½ CUPS

My basic marinara starts with a soffritto of onions, carrots and garlic. A soffritto, also called a battuto, is a base for many Italian sauces. If I'm adding meat to the marinara, I usually eliminate the carrots. If the sauce is to be used with fish, I'll add celery, parsley and crushed red pepper. In season, of course, you'll want to use fresh tomatoes. The longer the marinara simmers, the more flavorful it will become. I usually cook my marinara for about two hours over very low heat.

2 tablespoons extra virgin olive oil

½ cup chopped sweet onions

½ cup peeled, chopped carrots

1 tablespoon finely chopped garlic

½ cup dry red wine

2 28-ounce cans peeled whole tomatoes

1 teaspoon sea salt

½ teaspoon freshly ground black pepper

¼ teaspoon red pepper flakes

½ cup chopped basil

½ cup chopped Italian parsley

Heat the olive oil in a nonreactive saucepan over moderately low heat. Add the onions and carrots and sauté for about 10 minutes, stirring occasionally with a wooden spoon, until tender. Add the garlic and cook for just a minute or two. Don't let the garlic brown, or the sauce will taste like burnt garlic. Deglaze with the red wine and cook until reduced by half.

Puree the tomatoes through a food mill and add to the pan. Bring to a low simmer and stir in the salt, black pepper and red pepper flakes. Add the basil and parsley and simmer uncovered for at least 30 minutes, stirring occasionally to prevent the sauce from sticking. The sauce may be refrigerated for a week, and it keeps for months in the freezer.

# POTATO GNOCCHI

## WITH CHANTERELLES, ARUGULA AND TOMATO

Like gnudi, gnocchi are dumplings. But potatoes are the primary ingredient instead of cheese and eggs. They are delicious when served with spinach wilted in oil with a touch of minced garlic and topped with freshly grated Parmesan cheese. This version includes chanterelles, which elevate any dish in my book.

**FOR THE GNOCCHI**

1 pound russet potatoes

1¹/2 cups 00 flour

¹/2 teaspoon sea salt

¹/4 teaspoon grated fresh nutmeg

**FOR THE SAUCE**

1 tablespoon unsalted butter

12 ounces chanterelles, cleaned and trimmed

2 cups arugula, washed and stemmed

1 cup Marinara Sauce (page 98)

¹/4 teaspoon sea salt

¹/8 teaspoon freshly ground black pepper

Freshly grated Parmesan

Preheat the oven to 400°F. Pierce the potatoes several times with a sharp knife. Bake until tender, about 45 minutes. Using a kitchen towel to avoid burning your hands, remove the skins while the potatoes are still warm. Pass the peeled potatoes through a food mill or ricer, and spread out on a wooden board. Sift together the flour, salt and nutmeg, and spread evenly over the potatoes.

Gently incorporate the flour and seasonings into the riced potatoes, pressing the flour into the potatoes to form a mass. Do not knead it hard like bread; the gluten must not be developed in the flour lest the gnocchi be hard and chewy once cooked. Continue gathering the flour that falls off and pressing it into the potatoes until it creates a fairly cohesive mass.

Cover the dough with a towel and let it rest for 5 minutes. Using the palms of your hand, roll the dough into ropes about ¹/2 inch in diameter. Cut the logs into 1-inch pieces and dust with a little flour. Cook immediately or freeze until needed.

To make the sauce, melt the butter in a deep saucepan over low heat. Thinly slice the chanterelles. Add to the butter and increase the heat to moderate. Cook the chanterelles for about 3 minutes or until they soften and release their liquor. Stir in the arugula and cook for a few seconds, just until wilted. Add the marinara sauce and cook until warmed through. Remove the pan from the heat and season the sauce with the salt and pepper. Keep warm.

To cook the gnocchi, bring a large pot of salted water to a boil. Add the gnocchi and stir gently. They cook quickly: when they float to the surface, they're done. Gnocchi are fragile, so use a slotted spoon or spider strainer to carefully remove them from the boiling water.

Transfer immediately to the sauce, top with grated Parmesan and serve right away. They are best when steaming hot.

# HAZELNUT RAVIOLI
## WITH MINT BUTTER

Assembling ravioli is a relatively easy task once all of the ingredients have been assembled. The hazelnuts provide welcome texture and a toasty counterpoint to the richness of the cheese. They also add protein and nutritional balance to this exciting vegetarian dish. Goat's milk ricotta has a nice tang, but ricotta made from cow's or sheep's milk may be substituted.

**FOR THE FILLING**

2 pounds Goat's Milk Ricotta, drained, at room temperature

1/2 pound Parmesan, freshly grated

2 large egg yolks

1/3 cup blanched and peeled hazelnuts, lightly roasted and finely chopped

1 tablespoon sea salt

1 teaspoon freshly ground black pepper

**FOR THE RAVIOLI**

1 large egg

2 pounds Basic Pasta sheets (page 104)

1 pound filling

1 1/2 tablespoons Black Pepper-Mint Butter (page 123)

2 ounces dry sheep's milk cheese, such as caciocavallo, shaved

1 teaspoon blanched and peeled hazelnuts, toasted and crushed

To make the filling, combine the ricotta, Parmesan, egg yolks, hazelnuts, salt and pepper in a large mixing bowl. Using a wooden spoon or rubber spatula, begin blending the ingredients by folding them into each other. Slowly incorporate the ricotta a bit at a time until the mixture is smooth. Set aside and refrigerate until needed.

To make the ravioli, whisk the egg with 2 tablespoons water in a small bowl. Lay out one sheet of pasta on a lightly floured work surface.

Divide the ravioli filling in half, and from that spoon 2 tablespoons of filling into two evenly spaced rows of 8. Brush some of the egg wash around the mounds of filling. Carefully fit another sheet of pasta over the top, and press down using the tips of your fingers around the filling to remove the air and create a seal. For square or rectangular ravioli, use a scalloped pastry wheel to cut the dough. For round ravioli, use a small cookie cutter or a special ravioli cutter. Repeat with remaining dough and filling.

The ravioli may be cooked immediately. If reserving for later use, dust with flour to prevent sticking, then store in containers with tight lids and refrigerate or freeze.

To serve, cook 20 ravioli in salted boiling water until tender, 8 to 10 minutes. They will float to the top when they are ready. Melt the butter in a small pan over low heat, taking care not to brown the mint. Drain the ravioli and transfer to a warm serving bowl. Spoon on the butter and garnish with the cheese and nuts. Serve immediately.

## GOAT'S MILK RICOTTA

MAKES 1 POUND

Traditional ricotta utilizes the liquid, or whey, left over from cheese production after the curd has been strained. This is a simple recipe, though it takes a bit of time and patience. It is something we often make at the restaurant when our market has goat milk that is nearing its sell-by date. We use it to stuff pasta or as the base for our gnudi, but it is quite delicious when served on its own seasoned with some sea salt, black pepper and a little drizzle of your favorite oil as part of an antipasto.

Note that the recipe calls for cream that has not been ultrapasteurized, or super-heated, which can prevent the curds from developing since the cream has already been cooked beyond the temperature required to denature the protein.

2 quarts whole cow's milk

I cup goat's milk

I cup heavy cream
(not ultrapasteurized)

2 1/2 tablespoons fresh lemon juice

Pour both milks, cream and lemon juice into a large, nonreactive pot. Heat over low heat until the mixture reaches 194°F on a candy thermometer. This might take 1 to 2 hours.

Line a fine-mesh sieve with dampened cheesecloth. When curds form on the surface of the liquid, skim them from the top and transfer them to the sieve. Increase the heat to moderate and simmer for about 8 minutes. Keep skimming the curds and transferring them to the sieve until only milky liquid remains. Allow the curds to drain for at least 1 hour or until the desired consistency is achieved.

*(recipe continues)*

# BASIC PASTA

My former sous chef Alan Bergo used to make all of Heartland's pasta. This is his recipe, using the traditional "well and fork method" that my grandmother taught me when I was a boy. It's pretty simple. Alan likes to use a combination of semolina and all-purpose flours, which yields a dough that's light but resilient and easy to work with. We roll it into sheets for ravioli, which we make in quantity and freeze for later use, as you can do at home.

| | |
|---|---|
| I cup semolina flour | 2 eggs |
| I cup all-purpose flour | 1/4 cup warm water or sparkling water |
| 1/2 teaspoon sea salt | |

In a bowl, whisk together the flours and salt, and place in a mound on a wooden board. Use a fork to make a well in the center. Crack the eggs into the well.

Begin incorporating the flour with a fork. Work from the inner rim of the well, making sure to pull fresh flour from the lower part of the well, pushing the fresh flour under the dough. This helps keep the dough from sticking to the board.

As the eggs become fully absorbed, drizzle in a little water as needed to keep the dough from drying out and to help it form more evenly. If any pieces of dough stick to the fork, pull them loose and press them into the dough using your hands. Set the dough aside.

Scrape the board and discard any stuck-on pieces. (They cause lumps and holes when the dough is stretched.) Sprinkle a light dusting of fresh all-purpose flour on the board. Do not sprinkle flour on the dough. Start kneading the dough, using the palm of one hand while folding the dough over with the other hand. Knead the dough for 2 to 3 minutes. Cover with a towel and allow to rest for 30 minutes.

To roll out the pasta, flatten the dough ball with the palm of your hand so it fits between the rollers of your machine. Set the machine on it widest setting, and feed the dough through the machine with one hand while catching it with the other. Lightly flour the dough on one side and fold it into thirds. Repeat this process 8 to 10 times until the dough is smooth and elastic, flouring only if necessary to prevent sticking.

Adjust the machine to the next setting. Flour the dough on both sides and feed through the machine. Repeat while adjusting to progressively narrower settings; we always take pasta down to the lowest setting on the machine.

Lay the pasta out on lightly floured baking sheets and proceed to make some ravioli.

# DUCK LIVER RAVIOLI
## WITH MUSHROOMS AND SAGE CREAM

SERVES 4

This is based on my recipe for duck liver mousse with the addition of bread crumbs and egg to help prevent the filling from leaking out of the pasta as it cooks. I like to use unseasoned, finely textured Japanese-style panko here. Any game bird liver may be substituted for the duck's. Note that the livers must soak overnight.

**FOR THE STUFFING**

I pound duck livers or other game bird liver

Milk

1/3 pound unsalted butter (preferably high fat)

2 cups diced onions

1/4 cup sage, chopped

1/4 cup thyme leaves

I tablespoon sea salt

I tablespoon freshly ground black pepper

1/2 teaspoon ground nutmeg

2 cups panko

I egg

**FOR THE RAVIOLI**

I large egg

2 pounds Basic Pasta sheets

I pound filling

2 teaspoons unsalted butter

1/4 pound button mushrooms, trimmed and sliced

1/4 teaspoon sea salt

1/8 teaspoon freshly ground black pepper

I cup Sage Cream

12 fried sage leaves

To make the filling, soak the livers overnight in the refrigerator in a bowl of milk. Drain the livers and set aside. Heat the butter in a medium saucepan over moderately low heat. Add the onions and livers and stir in the herbs. Sweat without browning until the onions are translucent and the livers are cooked through, 5 to 7 minutes.

Pass the liver mixture through a food mill and set aside to cool to room temperature. Add the salt, pepper, nutmeg, panko and egg and blend until thoroughly combined. Refrigerate the stuffing, and allow it to set before stuffing the ravioli.

To make the ravioli, lay out one sheet of pasta on a lightly floured work surface. Whisk the egg with 2 tablespoons water in a small bowl.

*(recipe continues)*

Divide the ravioli filling in half, and from that spoon 1 ounce (2 tablespoons) of filling into two evenly spaced rows of 8. Brush some of the egg wash around the mounds of filling. Carefully fit another sheet of pasta over the top, and press down using the tips of your fingers around the filling to remove the air and create a seal. For square or rectangular ravioli, use a scalloped pastry wheel to cut the dough. For round ravioli, use a small cookie cutter or a special ravioli cutter. Repeat with remaining dough and filling.

The ravioli may be cooked immediately. If reserving for later use, dust with flour to prevent sticking, then store in containers with tight lids and refrigerate or freeze.

To serve, cook 20 ravioli in salted boiling water until tender, 8 to 10 minutes. They will float to the top when they are ready.

Melt the butter in a large skillet over moderately high heat. Add the mushrooms and pan roast until well browned, 8 to 10 minutes. Season with the salt and pepper. Reduce the heat to low. Add the sage cream.

Drain the ravioli and transfer to a warm serving bowl. Pour the sauce and mushrooms over the ravioli, and garnish with the fried sage. Serve immediately.

## SAGE CREAM

MAKES 3 CUPS

This sauce was created to accompany chicken, either pan fried or roasted, but it also makes the right pasta something extra-special. It is lightened with court-bouillon, while sherry contributes a nutty top note.

| | |
|---|---|
| I quart heavy cream | I teaspoon fine sea salt |
| 2 cups Court-Bouillon (page 268) | 1/2 teaspoon freshly ground white pepper |
| 1/2 cup cream sherry | |
| Bouquet garni (I bay leaf, 6 sprigs sage) | 2 tablespoons unsalted butter, softened |

Heat the cream and court-bouillon in a large saucepan over moderately low heat. Add the sherry and bouquet garni, season with the salt and pepper and simmer for 20 minutes, whisking occasionally to prevent scalding. Discard the bouquet garni. Remove from the heat. Whisk in the softened butter. Strain through a fine-mesh sieve lined with damp cheesecloth. Refrigerate until needed.

# VEGETABLES
*and*
# SIDE PLATES

On my way to Minnesota, passing from
state to state, I was astounded
by the magnificence of
America's agricultural might.

# VEGETABLES
*and*
# SIDE PLATES

---

ROASTED BEETS
with Preserved Cranberry Vinaigrette • 111

SUMMER VEGETABLE RAGOUT • 113

ASPARAGUS
with Mornay Sauce and Fried Egg • 114

KALE TORTE • 117

SWEET POTATO-ROOT VEGETABLE HASH • 120

MINT-SCENTED WILD MUSHROOMS • 123

BABY GREEN BEANS with Honey-Pecan Cream • 124

BRAISED RED CABBAGE • 125

FRESH VEGETABLE SLAW • 126

CAPONATA • 129

LEEK CONFIT • 130

BALSAMIC ROASTED SWEET ONIONS • 131

BRUSSELS SPROUTS
with Warm Pancetta Vinaigrette • 132

GRILLED RAMPS
with Tarragon Agrodolce • 133

ROMA TOMATO CONFIT • 136

MUSHROOM POTATO PUREE • 137

# ROASTED BEETS
## WITH PRESERVED CRANBERRY VINAIGRETTE

This simple but special side is good warm, cold or at room temperature. It's an autumn winter dish that draws on tart-sweet dried cranberries as the principal flavor.

3 pounds beets, preferably Chioggia, white and/or gold

I cup grapeseed oil

I cup Preserved Cranberry Vinaigrette

Preheat oven to 350°. Trim the ends of the beets so they sit upright. Rub with the oil, and stand on a baking sheet. Bake for 45 minutes or until easily pierced with a fork. Allow the beets to cool until they can be safely handled but are still warm. Rub with a kitchen towel to remove the skins. Thinly slice and toss with the Preserved Cranberry Vinaigrette.

## PRESERVED CRANBERRY VINAIGRETTE

MAKES 2½ CUPS

I cup dried cranberries

I teaspoon fine sea salt

¼ cup red wine vinegar

I tablespoon chopped fresh garlic, chopped

I tablespoon chopped fresh shallots, chopped

I tablespoon chopped Italian parsley, chopped

½ teaspoon freshly ground black pepper

1½ cups grapeseed or extra virgin olive oil

In a small bowl, combine the cranberries with just enough warm water to cover. Soak for 10 minutes. Transfer berries and soaking water to a blender and process to puree. Leave mixture in blender.

In a small bowl, dissolve the salt in the vinegar. Add to the cranberry puree with the garlic, shallots, parsley and pepper. Working on high speed, slowly add the oil in a thin stream until the dressing is emulsified. Cover and refrigerate any extra vinaigrette.

# SUMMER VEGETABLE RAGOUT

Light and buttery, this tumble of young spring vegetables makes an excellent side dish for grilled or pan-fried fish, or a special vegetarian entree when served with polenta and morels as shown.

Naturally, the ingredients you use will vary depending upon where you live. In Minnesota, asparagus can be an early summer crop if spring gets off to a late start. In any case, it's an elegantly simple way to enjoy the season's finest. Take care to trim all vegetables to approximately the same size, to ensure that they cook evenly. If you include asparagus tips in combination with baby root vegetables and tiny onions, add them halfway through so they don't overcook.

2 tablespoons unsalted butter

1/2 pound assorted summer vegetables such as asparagus tips, bunching onions, peas, radishes, baby leeks, baby carrots and button mushrooms, cleaned and trimmed

1 teaspoon chopped garlic

1/2 cup Court-Bouillon (page 268)

1/4 teaspoon sea salt

1/4 teaspoon freshly ground white pepper

2 teaspoons chopped Italian parsley

Melt 1 tablespoon butter in a medium saucepan over moderate heat. Add the vegetables and garlic and cook for 2 minutes, stirring occasionally.

Add the court-bouillon and stir gently. Cook until the vegetables are tender. Season with salt and pepper. Add the parsley. Stir in the remaining butter and serve.

# ASPARAGUS
## WITH MORNAY SAUCE AND FRIED EGG

We all deserve to indulge once in a while, and this combination is a great way to celebrate spring's local harvest. The sauce is a traditional French mornay made with milk, cream, eggs and cheese. Topping it with a fried egg might seem like overkill, but I think it's just what the doctor ordered. On second thought, it's so indulgent that the doctor probably wouldn't order it, but she'd doubtless find it difficult to resist.

| | |
|---|---|
| 1¹/2 sticks unsalted butter | 1¹/2 cups grated Swiss cheese |
| 6 tablespoons all-purpose flour | 4 egg yolks, beaten with 2 tablespoons of milk |
| 4 cups cold milk | |
| 2 teaspoons sea salt | ¹/4 cup heavy cream |
| 1 teaspoon freshly ground white pepper | 1¹/2 pounds asparagus, trimmed and blanched until tender |
| ¹/2 teaspoon ground nutmeg | 6 fried eggs |

To make the sauce, melt the butter in a medium saucepan over moderately low heat. Whisk in the flour until well blended, but don't let it brown. Add the cold milk, whisking to prevent lumps. Once it reaches a simmer, remove from the heat and pour the sauce through a fine-mesh strainer. Season with the salt, pepper and nutmeg. Return the sauce to the pan, set over low heat and gradually stir in the cheese until melted. Add the egg yolk mixture. Slowly bring the sauce to a boil while continuously whisking. Remove from the heat and add the cream. Set aside in a warm place.

To serve, divide the blanched asparagus among six warm serving plates. Ladle some of the sauce over the asparagus, and top each serving with a fried egg, seasoned with a little sea salt and freshly ground black pepper.

# KALE TORTE

This rich green tart takes basic kale to a whole new level. Serve it warm with marinara sauce, or top it with sautéed wild mushrooms. I think it's also delicious when eaten at room temperature.

Pâté brisée, or basic short dough of flour, butter, salt and water, is commonly used for crust. I substitute crème fraîche plus one whole egg for the water. I find this imparts a richer flavor and pleasing golden color to the crust. It also helps the dry ingredients cohere, which makes for an easier time when forming the dough. It is critical not to overcook the filling, or you'll end up with green scrambled eggs.

**FOR THE CRUST**

1 3/4 cups all-purpose flour

1/2 teaspoon sea salt

1/4 pound cold unsalted butter, cut into cubes

1 whole egg

1 teaspoon crème fraîche or sour cream

1/4 teaspoon freshly grated nutmeg

**FOR THE FILLING**

1 pound lacinato kale, ribs removed and julienned

2 teaspoons sea salt

1 quart heavy cream

1 cup grated Parmesan

4 large eggs

2 egg yolks

1 teaspoon sea salt

To make the crust, sift the flour into a large bowl and add the salt. Add the butter and work it into the flour with your fingertips until coarse, sand-like grains are formed. Push the mixture up the sides of the bowl, leaving enough in the bottom to allow you to dig a well in the center.

Crack the egg into the well. Using a fork, lightly beat the egg. Then, using a wooden spoon, incorporate the flour mixture little by little with the egg. Add the crème fraîche, and mix again until the dough is homogeneous. If it feels a little dry and difficult to work, add a few drops of water to make it more pliable. Transfer the dough to a lightly floured work surface. Using your hands, knead the dough for a few seconds until it forms a ball. Cover with plastic wrap and refrigerate for one hour. Remove the dough from refrigerator and allow it to warm to room temperature before proceeding.

*(recipe continues)*

Roll out the dough on a lightly floured work surface to an 11-inch round. Roll the dough up onto the rolling pin and transfer it to a 9-inch fluted tart pan with a removable base. Using a paring knife, trim the edges. Refrigerate for at least 30 minutes.

Preheat the oven to 375° F. Line the dough with parchment paper and fill with pie weights or dried beans. Bake the crust for 12 to 14 minutes or until it sets but is not browned. Remove the paper and weights, and return the crust to the oven. Bake for another 8 to 10 minutes or until golden brown. Remove from the oven and cool on a wire rack.

While the crust is cooling, bring a pot of salted water to the boil. Add the kale leaves and julienne stems and blanch until just wilted, then drain. Transfer the kale to an ice water bath to stop the cooking and help preserve the chlorophyll that is essential to this torte's deep green color.

Drain the kale, squeezing any excess water. Using a high-speed blender or food processor, purée the kale with the cream, parmesan, eggs, egg yolks and salt. Strain the mixture through a fine-mesh sieve to remove any lumps and stray bits of kale.

Reduce the oven temperature to 325° F. Pour the filling into the prebaked crust and bake for 20 to 25 minutes, until just set. You can check this by tapping lightly on the side of the pan to see if the filling trembles.

Remove the torte from the oven and allow it to cool slightly on a wire rack before removing it from the pan. Slice and serve immediately with a side salad.

# SWEET POTATO–ROOT VEGETABLE HASH

Serve this versatile, nourishing hash as a side dish for dinner or beneath a couple of fried duck eggs for breakfast. Since hash recipes evolved as a way to repurpose leftovers, feel free to use any combination of cooked root vegetables such as parsnip, carrot, celeriac, turnip, rutabaga, parsley root or salsify.

6 pounds sweet potatoes, peeled and diced

4 pounds assorted root vegetables, peeled and diced

3/4 cup diced sweet onions

2 tablespoons rendered duck fat or unsalted butter

2 teaspoons thyme leaves

2 teaspoons chopped Italian parsley

1/2 teaspoon sea salt

1/4 teaspoon freshly ground black pepper

Bring a large pot of salted water to a boil over high heat. Add the sweet potatoes and root vegetables and blanch for 5 to 7 minutes, until tender. Drain and cool thoroughly.

In a large skillet over moderate heat, melt the duck fat or butter. Add the sweet potatoes, root vegetables and onions and sauté for about 20 minutes, gently stirring to brown evenly, until tender. Using a wooden spoon to prevent breaking up the vegetables, gently stir in the thyme, parsley, salt and pepper. Serve immediately.

# MINT-SCENTED WILD MUSHROOMS

Redolent of spring, this fragrant herbal side dish is quick and easy to prepare. It was created to use our great local bounty of wild mushrooms such as chanterelles, but regular button mushrooms or an exotic cultivated mushroom such as crimini, shiitake or oyster work well too. It also makes a special treat for vegetarians.

| | |
|---|---|
| 3 ounces Black Pepper-Mint Butter | 1½ pounds wild mushrooms, cleaned and trimmed |

Heat the butter over moderate heat in a nonreactive pan. Add the mushrooms and sauté until tender. Adjust the seasoning if necessary. Serve immediately.

## BLACK PEPPER MINT BUTTER

MAKES 1 CUP

The recipe makes more than you need for the mushrooms, but it freezes well and is delicious on almost any plain steamed vegetable.

| | |
|---|---|
| ½ pound unsalted butter, at soft room temperature | ½ teaspoon sea salt |
| 1½ teaspoons chopped fresh mint | ½ teaspoon freshly ground black pepper |

Blend the butter, mint, salt and pepper in a food processor until smooth. Scrape into a container, cover tightly and refrigerate until ready to use.

# BABY GREEN BEANS
## WITH HONEY-PECAN CREAM

The difference between haricots verts and what we commonly call string beans is simply a matter of how long they are left on the vine. With luck, you might find the yellow variety, which are immature wax beans—sometimes called yellow filet beans. The advantage of harvesting and eating these beans when they are young is that they are amazingly tender.

This simple side dish is excellent with grilled or roast pork. It features a simple spiced reduction of heavy cream with honey and toasted pecans. Since they are already tender when raw, I like to blanch my haricots verts in salted boiling water for about two minutes and then immediately shock them in ice water before adding them to the reduction. In that way, I can be sure that the delicate beans do not overcook.

I cup heavy cream

I tablespoon sherry

I tablespoon honey

I bay leaf

I cinnamon stick

Pinch of freshly grated nutmeg

I teaspoon unsalted butter, at room temperature

2 tablespoons pecans, toasted and coarsely chopped

Sea salt and freshly ground white pepper to taste

1/2 pound haricots verts, trimmed and blanched

In a medium saucepan, warm the cream over moderately low heat. Add the sherry, honey, bay leaf, cinnamon and nutmeg and simmer for 20 minutes, whisking occasionally to prevent scalding.

Remove and discard the bay leaf and cinnamon stick. Remove the pan from the heat. Whisk in the softened butter, making sure it is well incorporated. Stir in the pecans and season to taste. Add the beans and return the pan to low flame. Heat for thirty seconds or until the beans are warmed through. Serve immediately.

# BRAISED RED CABBAGE

The cuisine of Central Europe informs the food of America's heartland, and it is the inspiration for this savory side dish, which is always welcome in cold weather. I prefer to prepare the cabbage with rendered duck fat since it is actually lighter than lard or butter, but use what you like. As a variation, add a skin-on, cored and sliced apple or a handful of raisins a minute or two before the cabbage finishes cooking.

2 tablespoons rendered duck fat, pork lard or unsalted butter

2 tablespoons chopped garlic

1 1/2 pounds red cabbage, cored and sliced

1/2 cup Court-Bouillon (page 268) or low-sodium vegetable broth

1 teaspoon sea salt

1/2 teaspoon freshly ground black pepper

1/2 teaspoon caraway seeds

Melt the fat in a large, nonreactive saucepan over moderate heat. Add the garlic and cabbage. Stir until the cabbage begins to wilt. Add the court-bouillon. Stir in the salt, pepper and caraway seeds. Continue cooking until the court-bouillon is nearly evaporated.

# FRESH VEGETABLE SLAW

No one considers slaw haute, but I have always enjoyed using different combinations of shredded vegetables and sometimes fruit in a light dressing as a garnish or accompaniment to more complicated preparations. Slaws go so well with a beautiful piece of fresh fish or grilled meat, and provide the kind of contrast I really enjoy. I often combine hot and cold ingredients when composing a dish.

The following recipes are essentially the same as far as basic seasonings and method of preparation, but the slight variations really do make a difference. Fennel-Cabbage Slaw is best with fish, while Apple-Fennel Slaw is meant to accompany chicken or pork.

I pound Savoy cabbage, cored and thinly sliced

I pound red cabbage, cored and thinly sliced

I pound turnips, finely julienned

I pound carrots, peeled and finely julienned

I pound sweet onions, thinly sliced

I cup apple cider vinegar

2 tablespoons fine sea salt

3 cups grapeseed oil

I tablespoon freshly ground black pepper

1/2 cup chopped flat leaf parsley

1/2 cup chopped tarragon leaves

Combine the cabbages, turnips, carrots and onions in a large nonreactive bowl and toss with your hands to combine.

In a small bowl, whisk together the vinegar and the salt. Whisk in the oil, pepper, parsley and tarragon. Pour over the slaw and toss well, making sure all of the ingredients are well blended.

## VARIATIONS ON A THEME

Follow the recipe for Fresh Vegetable Slaw, replacing the cabbages, turnips and carrots with equal amounts fall and winter produce.

### APPLE-FENNEL SLAW

5 pounds apples, cored and julienned

3 cups cored, shaved fresh fennel

3 cups thinly sliced red onions

### FENNEL-CABBAGE SLAW

5 pounds green cabbage, cored and thinly sliced

3 cups cored, shaved fresh fennel

3 cups thinly sliced red onions

# CAPONATA

I get so tired of people telling me they don't like eggplant. I grew up eating it, usually served casserole-style as eggplant Parmesan. Sometimes that eggplant Parmesan became a delicious sandwich. Most people think eggplant is a vegetable, but it is actually a berry in the nightshade family. If you don't believe me, take a blueberry and an eggplant, cut them in half and compare.

The following recipe may not change your life, but it might change your mind about eggplant. It's great on its own, as part of an antipasto plate or as a relish with grilled fish or chicken—even steak.

| | |
|---|---|
| 6 large eggplants, peeled and diced | 2 cups diced red onions |
| 1¹/₂ tablespoons sugar | 2 cups seeded and diced tomatoes |
| 2¹/₂ cups grapeseed oil, sunflower oil or extra virgin olive oil | 2 cups diced red bell peppers |
| 1¹/₂ teaspoons sea salt | ³/₄ cup red wine vinegar |
| 1¹/₂ teaspoons freshly ground black pepper | 1 cup brined capers, drained |
| 2 cups diced celery | ¹/₂ cup chopped basil |
| | ¹/₂ cup chopped Italian parsley |

Preheat the oven to 350°F. In a large bowl, combine the eggplant with the sugar, half of the oil, salt and pepper. Turn out the eggplant onto a large sheet pan and roast until tender, about 20 minutes.

Combine the remaining oil with the celery, onions, tomatoes, peppers, vinegar, capers, basil and parsley in a large bowl. Mix well. Add the eggplant and toss until fully incorporated.

# LEEK CONFIT

At Heartland we are always at work saving the best of each season's produce. The classic technique called confit allows us to cook vegetables in their summer prime for use during the winter. This leek confit is a terrific accompaniment to roast chicken—or even a grilled chicken breast in the heat of July.

12 medium leeks, white and light green parts only

1/2 pound unsalted butter

2 teaspoons sea salt

1 teaspoon freshly ground white pepper

2 tablespoons chopped chervil or tarragon

Cut the leeks into julienne strips and place in a bowl of cold water for about 10 minutes.

Bring a large pot of salted water to the boil over high heat. Add the leeks and blanch for 30 seconds, then drain.

Melt the butter in a large skillet over very low heat. Add the leeks, salt and pepper. Cook for 10 minutes, stirring occasionally. Remove from the heat, and stir in the chervil. The leeks may be used immediately, refrigerated for 2 weeks or frozen.

# BALSAMIC ROASTED SWEET ONIONS

SERVES 8 TO 10

Here's a simple but effective accompaniment to any roast meat. One of our local Minnesota wineries produces a balsamic vinegar aged in old wine barrels. It may not be the genuine article from Modena, but it's still pretty darn good. We also use house-fermented ice wine vinegar for this recipe. It imparts a flavor that's all our own.

48 baby sweet onions, peeled and quartered or halved if desired

I cup grapeseed oil

I cup balsamic vinegar

I tablespoon fine sea salt

1/2 teaspoon freshly ground white pepper

Preheat the oven to 350°F. In a large bowl, toss the onions in the oil and vinegar, and season with the salt and pepper. Roast for 25 minutes. Serve warm or at room temperature.

# BRUSSELS SPROUTS
## WITH WARM PANCETTA VINAIGRETTE

Brussels sprouts are one of our favorite cold crops. Having spent many years cooking on the East Coast where brussels sprouts were not, at the time, received with much enthusiasm, I was pleasantly surprised with the positive response when I put them on a menu here in the Midwest. We have extended access to them over the winter months, and they pair well with our house-cured bacon and pancetta. This recipe reflects that happy marriage.

2 tablespoons unsalted butter

3 pounds brussels sprouts, trimmed of outer leaves and halved

1/2 teaspoon sea salt

1/4 teaspoon freshly ground black pepper

2 cups Court-Bouillon (page 268) or vegetable broth

2 cups Pancetta Vinaigrette (page 261)

Heat the butter in a large pot over moderate heat. Add the brussels sprouts and season with the salt and pepper. Cook until lightly browned. Pour in the court-bouillon and cover with a tight-fitting lid. Simmer until tender, about 7 minutes.

Drain the brussels sprouts, discarding the court-bouillon, and return them to the pan. Add the vinaigrette and heat over a low flame until warmed through. Serve immediately.

# GRILLED RAMPS
## WITH TARRAGON AGRODOLCE

I return to my Italian heritage for this very simple preparation of grilled ramps (wild leeks). It works just as well with baby leeks or scallions. The sauce is an agrodolce, or piquant Italian sweet and sour sauce I find irresistible.

I pound ramps, trimmed

2 tablespoons grapeseed oil

1/2 teaspoon sea salt

1/4 teaspoon freshly ground black pepper

3/4 cup Tarragon Agrodolce, warmed

Preheat a grill to high. In a large bowl, combine the ramps with the oil and toss to coat well. Season with the salt and pepper.

Lightly grill the ramps over a very hot flame until tender and slightly browned, about 2 minutes. Transfer to a platter and dress with the agrodolce.

## TARRAGON AGRODOLCE

This traditional sauce has a very literal translation: agro (sour) and dolce (sweet). It's good with chicken, fish and grilled vegetables, and keeps well refrigerated for 2 weeks.

2 tablespoons grapeseed oil

I cup minced shallots

3 tablespoons sugar

2 cups white wine

I cup red wine vinegar

I cup golden raisins

I tablespoon sea salt

1/2 tablespoon freshly ground white pepper

1/2 cup chopped tarragon

Heat the oil in a medium saucepan over moderate heat. Add the shallots and sugar and cook until translucent, about 5 minutes. Add the wine, vinegar and raisins, and increase the heat. Bring to a boil, stirring occasionally.

Reduce the heat, and simmer the sauce for 2 minutes. Remove from the heat and stir in the salt, pepper and tarragon.

# ROMA TOMATO CONFIT

Summer tomatoes preserved at their prime are a treat when eaten a few months later. This robust confit is great with fish or as a topping for pizza. It also makes a tasty condiment for sandwiches in lieu of fresh tomatoes. Be sure to reserve the savory oil after removing the tomatoes. Toss it with pasta or drizzle over toasted crusty bread.

2 pounds Roma or other plum tomatoes, cored and halved lengthwise

6 garlic cloves

I tablespoon sea salt

1/2 tablespoons freshly ground black pepper

2 cups grapeseed oil, sunflower oil or extra virgin olive oil

Preheat the oven to 400°F. Place the tomatoes and garlic in a baking dish. Season with the salt and pepper. Pour the oil over top.

Cover tightly with foil and roast for 30 minutes. Remove the tomatoes from the oven, and carefully remove the foil, making sure to release the steam away from your face. Cool to room temperature and transfer to a jar or container with a tight lid. Pour in the oil, making sure the tomatoes are completely covered with it. Use immediately or refrigerate for up to 3 months.

# MUSHROOM POTATO PURÉE

This rich, earthy variation on basic potato purée is enormously popular whenever we serve it at the restaurant. It's a dream of a side dish that elevates any simple roast meat or fish.

6 large golden potatoes, peeled and quartered (about 2 pounds)

3/4 cup heavy cream

1/4 pounds unsalted butter

I cup Mushroom Duxelles

I tablespoon sea salt

1/2 tablespoon freshly ground white pepper

Bring a large pot of salted water to the boil. Add the potatoes, reduce the heat to moderate and cook until tender but not falling apart, about 15 minutes.

Drain the potatoes and transfer to a large bowl or a stand mixer fitted with the paddle attachment. Heat the cream and butter in a small saucepan. Add the cream mixture, mushroom duxelles, salt and pepper to the potatoes. Working on low speed or using a hand mixer, mash the potatoes until smooth and well combined.

## MUSHROOM DUXELLES

MAKES ABOUT 1 CUP

We use a lot of mushrooms at Heartland, and we also try to never waste anything. This French kitchen basic uses all the leftover stems and pieces after we trim mushrooms for other dishes. Mushroom duxelles may be stirred into risotto and pasta with dependably delicious results.

I tablespoon diced shallots

2 teaspoon unsalted butter

1/2 pound finely chopped button mushrooms, including stems

I tablespoon sherry

2 teaspoons thyme leaves

I teaspoon sea salt

1/2 teaspoon freshly ground black pepper

Melt the butter in a medium saucepan over moderate heat and add the shallots. Sweat until translucent, about 5 minutes. Add the mushrooms and sauté until they are almost dry. Add the sherry and stir to deglaze. Cook until the sherry evaporates. Add the thyme, salt and pepper. Remove the duxelles from the heat, allow it to cool and transfer to a jar or container with a tight lid. Refrigerate until ready to use.

# FRESHWATER FISH

During spawning season we make
caviar with local sturgeon
eggs gathered from roe sacs and
treated with sea salt.

# FRESHWATER FISH

GRILLED WHITEFISH
with Garlic Braised Spinach and Trout Roe Sour Cream • 141

FRESHWATER BOUILLABAISSE
with Rouille Toasts • 143

GRILLED STURGEON
with Lobter Mushrooms, Crayfish and Tarragon • 145

POACHED WHITEFISH
with Rhubarb Butter Sauce • 146

PAN FRIED RAINBOW TROUT
with Roasted Morels and Shell Pea-Mint Sauce • 149

HAZELNUT-CRUSTED LAKE CISCO
with Micro Greens Salad • 153

GRILLED LAKE TROUT
with Braised Turnip Greens and Yogurt Sauce • 154

# GRILLED WHITEFISH

## WITH GARLIC BRAISED SPINACH AND TROUT ROE SOUR CREAM

The Great Lakes whitefish is a salmonoid deriving its name from its silvery color. Fresh whitefish has a delicate flavor, and we usually serve it cured and smoked. Here it's grilled for a real treat.

I cup sour cream

I teaspoon freshly ground
black pepper

4 tablespoons trout roe (substitute
salmon roe or your favorite caviar)

6 whitefish filets (4-6 ounces each),
boneless

2 tablespoons grapeseed oil

2 teaspoons sea salt

I teaspoon freshly ground
white pepper

1 1/2 cups Carrot-Fennel Broth
(page 191)

Garlic Braised Spinach

In a medium bowl, mix the sour cream and black pepper until well blended. Fold in the roe, being careful not to break the eggs. Refrigerate until needed.

Preheat a grill to medium. Rub the whitefish filets on both sides with grapeseed oil, and season with salt and white pepper.

Grill the fish, turning once, until cooked through, about 6 minutes per side. To serve, ladle 1/4 cup of carrot-fennel broth into six shallow bowls. Add the spinach and top with a whitefish filet. Garnish with a dollop of trout roe sour cream.

## CARLIC BRAISED SPINACH

MAKES ABOUT 1 CUP

I tablespoon unsalted butter

2 garlic cloves, minced

6 cups spinach leaves, stemmed

1/2 teaspoon sea salt

1/4 teaspoon freshly ground
black pepper

1/2 teaspoon ground nutmeg

I cup Court-Bouillon (page 268)
or vegetable broth

Heat the butter in a saucepan over moderately low heat. Add the garlic and sweat until soft, about 1 minute. Add the spinach. Season with salt, pepper and nutmeg, and pour in the court-bouillon. Cover and braise until wilted, about 2 minutes.

# FRESHWATER BOUILLABAISSE
## WITH ROUILLE TOASTS

On our first visit to France, my wife and I stayed with friends in Marseille. We immediately went out to find authentic bouillabaisse, the signature local dish, and that led us to Chez Michel, a classic restaurant on the Mediterranean. We were greeted by a diminutive, elderly man, jaunty in an old-time French sailor's suit. It may have been a tourist trap, but we were swayed by the mounds of fresh fish, gills still gasping for air, piled high on crushed ice.

The bouillabaisse was spectacular, and I studied the contents of my plate in an effort to decode what I was eating. Here is my Midwestern adaptation of that meal using freshwater fish in place of ocean fish. I hope that it conveys the spirit of the classic.

**FOR THE ROUILLE**

1 roasted red bell pepper, seeded and peeled

2 garlic cloves

1 egg yolk

1 tablespoon Dijon mustard

2 tablespoons lemon juice

1/4 teaspoon sea salt

Pinch freshly ground white pepper

1/2 cup grapeseed oil

**FOR THE BOUILLABAISSE**

1 cup Fish Fumet (page 271) or seafood stock

2 tablespoons julienned leeks

1/4 cup julienned fennel

1/4 cup peeled, chopped tomatoes

1/4 teaspoon chopped garlic

1/2 teaspoon finely chopped Italian parsley

Pinch orange zest

1 teaspoon orange juice

Pinch saffron

1/2 teaspoon sea salt

1/4 teaspoon freshly ground black pepper

1/2 pound mixed firm white freshwater fish filets, including skinless whitefish, bass and lake trout

6 small (1-inch) baby potatoes

1/4 cup cooked and cleaned crayfish (substitute coarsely chopped cooked shrimp or lobster)

Toasted baguette slices

To make the rouille, combine the red pepper, garlic, egg yolk, mustard, lemon juice, salt and pepper in a food processor and puree until smooth. With the motor running, slowly add the oil in a thin stream until the sauce is emulsified.

*(recipe continues)*

To make the bouillabaisse, warm the fish fumet in a large skillet over moderate heat. Add the leeks, fennel, tomatoes, garlic, parsley, orange zest and juice, saffron, salt and pepper. Simmer for 8 minutes. Add the fish filets and potatoes. Simmer for 6 minutes. Add the crayfish and remove the pan from the heat. Allow to rest for 1 minute before serving. Divide the bouillabaisse evenly among serving bowls. Spread each baguette toast with a teaspoon of the rouille and serve with the soup.

## FROM THE HEARTLAND'S WATERS

Here in the Midwest, we have access to some very delicious freshwater fish. Most of the fish we serve at Heartland comes from Lake Superior. I usually get a call from someone who has just arrived at the dock at the lake's North Shore with a report of what's available. Then I order my fish and have it drop shipped for arrival the next day.

We also get fresh fish from Native Americans who fish the inland lakes, as well as from local farmers who raise trout, bass and perch. Occasionally, we get lake fish from Michigan, Ontario, Erie or Huron, through a regional broker.

Currently, crayfish are our only local shellfish, but I am working with my friend Chad Hebert on his freshwater lobster program. We hope to see the first harvest in the near future. For caviar, we rely on local sturgeon, paddlefish, lake cisco, salmon and trout. During spawning season, we often make our own caviar from eggs we gather from roe sacs and then treat with sea salt.

# GRILLED STURGEON

## WITH LOBSTER MUSHROOMS, CRAYFISH AND TARRAGON

SERVES 6

Like salmon and other fatty cold-water fish, sturgeon is as appealing when grilled as it is pan-roasted. The dense meat is interspersed with layers of yellow fat that provide insulation in cold northern waters. Rich and flavorful, a small amount of sturgeon goes a long way, so 4 or 5 ounces per person is plenty. Make sure that the fish is completely cooked through. Sturgeon is not a fish to eat medium rare, and its fat content permits thorough cooking without the meat becoming too dry. Do not try to eat the skin.

Once endangered, lake sturgeon has rebounded to the extent that regulated fishing is permitted in parts of Minnesota, Wisconsin and Michigan, including a brief Native American spearfishing season in Lake Winnebago, Wisconsin. Still, most sturgeon we serve is farm-raised. Paddlefish is a close relative, and like sturgeon, it produces a very desirable roe.

| | |
|---|---|
| 6 4-ounce boneless sturgeon steaks, about 1 inch thick, with skin on | ³/4 cup dry white wine |
| Grapeseed oil | 1¹/2 cups Crayfish Stock (page 272) or seafood stock |
| Sea salt and freshly ground black pepper to taste | 1¹/2 cups Fish Fumet (page 271) or more seafood stock |
| 2 tablespoons unsalted butter | 36 cooked, cleaned and shelled crayfish tails (substitute shrimp) |
| ¹/2 pound lobster mushrooms, cleaned and sliced | 1 teaspoon chopped tarragon leaves |
| 2 teaspoons minced garlic | ¹/2 teaspoon sea salt |
| 2 teaspoons minced shallots | ¹/4 teaspoon freshly ground white pepper |

Preheat the grill to medium. Brush the sturgeon on both sides with oil and season with salt and pepper. Grill until cooked through, about 8 minutes per side.

Melt 1 tablespoon of butter in a large skillet over moderate heat and add the mushrooms, garlic and shallots. Cook, stirring occasionally, for about 5 minutes. Stir in the wine and cook until it evaporates. Add the stock and fumet and cook until reduced by half. Add the crayfish and tarragon. Remove from the heat, whisk in the remaining butter and season with salt and pepper. Transfer the sturgeon to serving bowls and spoon on the sauce. Serve immediately.

# POACHED WHITEFISH
## WITH RHUBARB BUTTER SAUCE

Here in Minnesota, almost everyone has rhubarb growing somewhere in their yards, or in a neighbor's yard. Tales of rhubarb left in unlocked cars are common. No one wants to see this midsummer treat go to waste. Many people think rhubarb is a fruit. In fact, it's an herbaceous perennial vegetable, and this recipe uses it that way, as nature intended.

12 tablespoons unsalted butter, divided

3 rhubarb stalks, about 6 inches long, trimmed and chopped

1 large carrot, peeled and chopped

1/2 large fennel bulb, trimmed and chopped

1 medium leek (white part only), chopped

1 tablespoon thinly sliced fresh ginger

Bouquet garni (3 parsley sprigs, 3 springs lemon balm, 10 fragrant black peppercorns)

1 bottle (750 ml) full-bodied dry white wine such as chardonnay or pinot blanc

1 cup cold water

1 teaspoon fine sea salt

1/2 teaspoon freshly ground white pepper

4 4-ounce boneless whitefish filets, skin on and scaled

2 cups braised chard, for serving

Heat 2 tablespoons of butter in a wide saucepan over moderate heat. Add the rhubarb, carrot, fennel, leek and ginger and sweat until tender, about 5 minutes. Reserve 1 cup of the wine and pour the remaining wine into the pan. Add the bouquet garni. Bring to a boil, then reduce the heat and simmer for 25 minutes. Strain through a fine-mesh sieve and return the broth to the pan. Discard the vegetables and bouquet garni.

Add the fish in a single layer. Cover and bring to a boil, then reduce to a simmer. Cook until the fish is just cooked through, 6 to 8 minutes depending on the thickness of the filets. Carefully transfer the filets to a plate and keep warm. If desired, brush the fish with some melted butter to help keep them from drying out.

Strain the broth into a clean pan and bring to a boil. Add the remaining cup of wine. Reduce the heat to a simmer and cook the broth until reduced by half. Whisk in the remaining butter, 1 tablespoon at a time, until the sauce emulsifies. Remove from the heat, continuing to whisk until it stops simmering.

Divide the braised chard among serving plates. Place a filet on each serving of greens, dress it with the sauce and serve immediately.

# PAN FRIED RAINBOW TROUT
## WITH ROASTED MORELS AND SHELL PEA-MINT SAUCE

SERVES 6

This colorful dish celebrates our state mushroom, with first-of-the-season peas and mint. A small amount of butter adds rich flavor, while grapeseed oil prevents the butter from burning. The bright green sauce is so delicious that I often serve it to vegans as a vibrant spring soup. Try it with any white fish.

I cup morels

I tablespoon sunflower oil

1/2 teaspoon sea salt

1/4 teaspoon freshly ground
black pepper

1/2 cup all-purpose flour

1/2 teaspoon sea salt

1/4 teaspoon freshly ground
white pepper

6 8-ounce rainbow trout filets,
pin bones removed

I tablespoon grapeseed oil

I tablespoon unsalted butter

Shell Pea-Mint Sauce

Preheat oven to 350°F. On a small baking sheet, toss the morels with the oil, salt and pepper. Roast until tender, about 5 minutes.

In shallow bowl, combine the flour, salt and pepper. Dust the trout on both sides with the flour. Heat the oil in a large skillet over moderately high heat and add the butter. When it melts, carefully add the trout filets. Cook, turning once, for about 2 minutes per side. To serve, spoon warm pea sauce on the plate, top with trout and a few morels.

## SHELL PEA-MINT SAUCE

MAKES 2 CUPS

I cup shell peas, shucked

2 cups Court-Bouillon (page 268)
or vegetable broth

I cup extra virgin olive oil

1/2 cup mint leaves

1/2 cup Italian parsley leaves

2 teaspoons sea salt

1/2 teaspoon freshly ground
white pepper

Blanch the peas in salted boiling water until tender, about 3 minutes. Shock in a bowl of ice water then drain and transfer to a blender or food processor. Add the court-bouillon, olive oil, mint, parsley, salt and pepper. Blend on high speed until smooth.

# BULLFROG FARM FISH FARM

## MENOMONIE, WISCONSIN

———

In 1987, in Wisconsin's beautiful Chippewa Valley, Herby Radmann made a chance discovery of pure and plentiful water. Located just below the surface of some marginal farmland, the presence of an aquifer, along with Herby's vision, inspired the idea of sustainable fish farming. Armed with a dream and a rural legacy of determination and hard work, Herby, who calls himself the "Soul Proprietor," founded not only a farm in 1994, but also a community resource. Today, Bullfrog Farm produces upward of 20,000 pounds of rainbow trout each year.

Heartland takes weekly deliveries of Bullfrog Farm rainbow trout all year long. From July until October, when Herby is working with local trappers, we receive large quantities of freshwater crayfish. At our request, in recent years, Herby and his crew have also raised brook trout for us. While the brooks are much slower growing, their superior flavor profile makes them a special addition to our menu.

Everyone involved with Bullfrog is proud of working at a sustainable farm that holds the land and its resources in the highest regard. They also work toward the wellbeing of the community and understand the economic responsibilities associated with that. As Herby likes to say, "We work part time, but it takes all day."

# HAZELNUT-CRUSTED LAKE CISCO
## WITH MICRO GREENS SALAD

Lake cisco, or tullibee, is a salmonoid fish found in Lake Superior and other northern waters. They provide food for larger fish and hungry diners as well. There is genuine concern that the voracious and invasive Asian carp will find its way into the waters where lake cisco live, which would be devastating for the Great Lakes fishing industry. But for now, cisco are in great abundance, and we use both the fish and its roe in in many ways.

One tasty example is this dish, which calls for crayfish stock reduced with tomato concentrate to create a light sauce. The delicate salad plays off the hearty hazelnut crust.

2 tablespoons grapeseed oil

2 tablespoons butter

8 ounces hazelnut meal

12 3-ounce portions boneless lake cisco filet, skin on

Sea salt and freshly ground white pepper to taste

1¹/2 cups Crayfish Reduction, seasoned and warmed

³/4 pound micro greens

1 teaspoon lemon juice

1 teaspoon grapeseed oil

Heat the oil and butter in a large skillet over moderate heat. Place the hazelnut meal in a shallow bowl and season with salt and pepper. Coat the cisco with the hazelnut meal, turning it to encrust both sides. Place the cisco flesh side down in the hot pan. Cook, turning once, about 2 minutes per side.

Toss the greens with lemon juice, oil, salt and pepper. To serve, divide the sauce among six serving bowls, place the fish on the sauce and top with salad.

## CRAYFISH REDUCTION

¹/2 cup brandy

1 quart Crayfish Stock (page 272)

¹/4 cup tomato concentrate

¹/4 teaspoon sea salt

¹/4 teaspoon freshly ground black pepper

In a medium saucepan, heat the brandy over high heat and cook until reduced by half. Add the stock and tomato concentrate. Reduce the heat to a simmer. Simmer until syrupy and reduced by half, about 1 hour. Season with salt and pepper.

# GRILLED LAKE TROUT
## WITH BRAISED TURNIP GREENS AND YOGURT SAUCE

To run a profitable restaurant, it is imperative not to let food to go waste. It's the chef's challenge to use as much of an ingredient as possible, and elevate it to something special. Often, all that takes is combining it with another ingredient that complements it. I love those moments of culinary inspiration. This recipe uses the leafy tops of the many varieties of turnips we begin to see in late summer. The yogurt sauce does an admirable job of taming the spiciness of the greens.

**FOR THE TROUT**

6 lake trout filets (4 to 6 ounces each)

2 tablespoons grapeseed oil

2 teaspoons sea salt

1 teaspoon freshly ground white pepper

**FOR THE SAUCE**

1 1/2 cups plain low-fat yogurt

2 green onions, coarsely chopped

2 tablespoons chopped fresh dill

2 tablespoons grapeseed oil

1 tablespoon freshly squeezed lemon juice

1 teaspoon sea salt

1/2 teaspoon freshly ground black pepper

**FOR THE GREENS**

1 tablespoon unsalted butter

2 garlic cloves, minced

6 cups turnip greens, stemmed

1/2 teaspoon sea salt

1/4 teaspoon freshly ground black pepper

1/2 teaspoon ground nutmeg

1 cup Court-Bouillon (page 268)

Preheat a grill to moderate heat. Rub the trout on both sides with grapeseed oil and season it with the salt and white pepper. Grill the trout, about 6 minutes per side, until medium rare. Keep warm until ready to serve.

In a medium bowl, combine the yogurt, onions, dill, oil, lemon juice, salt and pepper and stir to mix well.

Melt the butter in a large saucepan over moderately low heat. Add the garlic and sweat until soft, about 1 minute. Add the greens. Season with salt, pepper and nutmeg, and pour in the court-bouillon. Cover and braise until wilted, about 3 minutes.

Divide the braised greens among six serving plates, and top each with a trout filet. Spoon a dollop of sauce alongside the fish and serve.

# MEAT
*and*
# GAME

We work hard in the kitchen
to make sure that every delicious bit
of our farmers' animals, head to tail,
is put to good use.

# MEAT
*and*
# GAME

---

GRILLED HERITAGE PORK CHOP
with Sweet Corn Relish • 159

PORK AND BLACK BEAN STEW • 164

OSSO BUCO
with Pumpkin Barley Risotto • 167

OXTAIL STEW with Dark Beer • 168

GRILLED VEAL RIB CHOP
with Tart Cherry Sausage and Preserved Cherry Glace • 169

SMOKED BEEF SIRLOIN
with Morels and Dandelion Greens • 172

IOWA SNAPPING TURTLE POT-AU-FEU • 175

WILD BOAR RAGÙ with Polenta • 177

ELK ROAST with Blackberry Glace and
Toasted Walnut Wild Rice • 178

GRILLED BISON TENDERLOIN
with Pumpkin Seed Pistou • 183

VENISON PORTERHOUSE CHOP
with Plums, Zinfandel and Rosemary • 185

HUNTER-STYLE RABBIT • 186

# GRILLED HERITAGE PORK CHOP
## WITH SWEET CORN RELISH

SERVES 6

Known in these parts as "The Great Minnesota Get-Together," the Minnesota State Fair is a righteous and beloved tradition. As a longtime member of the Minnesota Farmers Union, I have volunteered over the years to do cooking demonstrations at the state fair to help local farmers promote the food they grow. I demonstrated this simple, timeless summer recipe in 2003, before the great new interest in heritage breed pork. The chops we serve at Heartland are often from Duroc, a medium-sized American heirloom breed of pig that tastes fantastic.

6 heritage breed pork chops, preferably rib chops

3 tablespoons grapeseed oil

3 teaspoons fine sea salt

3/4 teaspoon freshly ground black pepper

2 1/2 tablespoons chopped fresh rosemary

2 1/2 tablespoons chopped fresh lavender

6 ears sweet corn, shucked

3 teaspoons fine sea salt

3 tablespoons apple cider vinegar

3 tablespoons grapeseed oil

1 1/2 tablespoons walnut oil

1/3 cup chopped sweet onions

1/3 cup bias-sliced green onions

1 1/2 teaspoons minced garlic

3 tablespoons chopped fresh rosemary

3/4 teaspoon freshly ground black pepper

Brush the pork chops on both sides with the grapeseed oil and season with salt, pepper, rosemary and lavender. Set aside.

Cut the corn kernels from the cobs, and cook the kernels in salted boiling water for 7 minutes. While the corn is cooking, dissolve the salt in the vinegar in a large nonreactive bowl. Whisk in the oils. Drain the corn, and add it to bowl with the onions, garlic, rosemary and pepper. Mix to combine and set aside.

Preheat the grill to medium. Grill the chops over direct heat for 6 minutes per side. To serve, spoon some corn relish onto six serving plates, and place a pork chop on top.

# THE MEAT MATTERS

A while back I saw a sign on a popular steakhouse that trumpeted their corn-fed beef. I suggested that they replace it with one reading "We don't care about you, the quality of life of these animals or the environment."

At Heartland, we require that the farmers who supply our meat raise their livestock in a humane fashion. This means animals raised on pasture rather than in confinement. We never procure animals treated with antibiotics, and all of the ruminants (animals that chew their cud) that we cook and serve here are fed what they were evolved to eat: grass.

Why have we always insisted on these standards? Animals that never evolved to eat grain cannot efficiently process its proteins. The latest dietary trend has people shunning gluten due to difficulty some individuals have in absorbing the proteins in certain grains. If you know someone who experiences discomfort after eating food containing gluten, you can understand the discomfort a ruminant feels when forced to consume grain.

I have witnessed firsthand the difference between cattle raised on grass and those raised on grain. As a member of the Minnesota Department of Agriculture Organic Advisory Task Force, I visited the branch campus of the Minnesota State University in Moorhead. The 100 percent grass-fed cattle were docile, nuzzling me as I walked through the pasture. Cattle raised on 100 percent grain in confinement were clearly in discomfort.

When grains are fed to ruminants, their ability to combat naturally occurring bacteria is compromised, and the results find their way into ground water and our food. In addition, the ratio of beneficial omega-3 fatty acids to omega-6 fatty acids in grain-fed meat is decreased. What should be a healthful protein becomes an unhealthful one and contributes to increased risk of illness for those who consume it. I encourage people to become more aware about the sources of their food, and to support farmers who act responsibly.

# PORK AND BLACK BEAN STEW

This hearty stew should serve you well during a long, cold winter, but if you live in a warm climate, it is just as appealing when enjoyed with an ice-cold beer. It feeds a crowd, tastes better when made a day or two in advance and freezes well.

5 pounds diced sweet onions

10 garlic cloves

I cup rendered duck fat

10 pounds diced lean pork

2 teaspoons cayenne pepper

I tablespoon paprika

2 tablespoons ground cumin

1 1/2 teaspoons ground cinnamon

I pound cooked Black Beans

I quart Brown Veal Stock (page 269)

2 cups reserved bean cooking water

4 plum tomatoes or 6 large tomatoes, seeded and chopped

2 tablespoons tomato concentrate

I bouquet garni (parsley sprig, thyme sprig, bay leaf and 1/2 whole nutmeg)

I tablespoon sea salt

I tablespoon freshly ground black pepper

In a very large dutch oven or stew pot, brown the onions and garlic in the duck fat over moderately high heat. Add the pork, cayenne, paprika, cumin and cinnamon. Cook for 10 minutes until the pork is well browned, then add the beans. Pour in the stock and the reserved cooking liquid. When the stew begins to simmer, stir in the tomatoes and tomato concentrate. Add the bouquet garni, and season with the salt and pepper. Cover and continue to simmer for 1 hour. Remove the bouquet garni before serving.

## BLACK BEANS

MAKES ABOUT 3 QUARTS

If your butcher doesn't have smoked pork hocks, substitute lean smoked bacon.

I pound black beans, rinsed and checked for stones

I small smoked pork hock

I sweet onion, peeled and studded with cloves

I carrot, peeled

I bouquet garni (parsley sprig, thyme sprig, bay leaf, garlic clove, 1/2 cinnamon stick and 5 black peppercorns)

Soak the beans overnight in twice their volume of water. Drain the beans, and place in a large pot with the pork hock, onion, carrot and bouquet garni. Pour in enough cold water to cover the beans by twice their volume.

Bring to a boil over high heat. Reduce to a simmer, and gently cook the beans until they are tender but not splitting, about 1½ hours. Add more water as needed to ensure that the beans remain soupy. Drain the beans, reserving the cooking liquid. Remove onions, carrots and the bouquet garni. Turn the beans out onto sheet pans and allow them to cool. Pull the meat off the pork hocks and add the meat to the beans.

# OSSO BUCO
## WITH PUMPKIN BARLEY RISOTTO

SERVES 8

This variation on a classic Italian dish uses ingredients from our regional farms. Barley, grown in the Upper Midwest and processed at Natural Way Mills in Middle River, Minnesota, takes the place of more traditional rice. Meaty autumn pumpkin gives a bit of sweetness, as does a classic mirepoix.

8 center-cut veal shanks (about I pound each with the bone), trussed

I cup all-purpose flour, seasoned with salt and pepper

9 tablespoons unsalted butter

I cup dry white wine

2 pounds diced onion, celery and carrots (mirepoix)

16 garlic cloves, peeled

3 1/2 pounds cored and chopped fresh or canned tomatoes

I gallon Brown Veal Stock (page 269)

Bouquet garni (3 rosemary sprigs, 3 thyme sprigs, 2 bay leaves, 24 black peppercorns and 6 whole cloves)

2 teaspoons sea salt

I teaspoon freshly ground black pepper

Roasted Pumpkin Barley Risotto (page 86)

Reserved braising liquid

To prepare the osso buco, pat the shanks with paper towels; they will brown better if they are dry. Dredge the shanks in the seasoned flour. Melt the butter in a large pot, add the shanks and brown on all sides. Deglaze with the white wine. Add the mirepoix, garlic, tomatoes, brown stock and bouquet garni. Cover and simmer over low heat until the shanks are tender, 2 to 3 hours. Season with the salt and pepper. Remove the bouquet garni. Remove the shanks and keep warm in a serving dish. Strain the braising liquid through a fine mesh sieve lined with dampened cheesecloth. Keep warm.

Prepare the Roasted Pumpkin Barley Risotto.

To serve, divide the risotto evenly among warm serving bowls. Place one shank on each serving of risotto, and spoon some hot braising liquid over the top.

# OXTAIL STEW
## WITH DARK BEER

To fully appreciate this dish, you must be prepared to luxuriate in the awesome fattiness of oxtails. The fat is meltingly sweet and rich—not something you would want to eat every day. However, oxtails are a magnificent excess that won't break the bank. Note that they should be soaked in cold water for several hours before cooking.

**FOR THE OXTAILS**

24 small oxtails

I cup all-purpose flour, seasoned with salt and pepper

¼ pound butter

I pound mirepoix (finely chopped celery, onion and carrots)

I pint dark beer

4 quarts Brown Veal Stock (page 269)

Bouquet garni (3 rosemary sprigs, I bay leaf, 12 black peppercorns and I whole nutmeg)

I tablespoon sea salt

2 teaspoons freshly ground pepper

**FOR THE STEW**

3 pounds assorted chopped vegetables including carrots, turnips, mushrooms and cipollini onions

I pound bacon, chopped

2 teaspoons sea salt

½ teaspoon freshly ground pepper

3 quarts reserved braising liquid from oxtails

Chopped fresh parsley for garnish

To prepare the oxtails, soak them in cold water for 3 to 4 hours. Drain and pat dry. Dust the oxtails with the seasoned flour. Melt the butter in a large dutch oven over moderately high heat and add the oxtails in two batches if necessary. Sear until well browned. Add the mirepoix, beer, brown stock and bouquet garni. Reduce the heat to low and simmer until the oxtails are tender, 3 to 4 hours. Season with the salt and pepper. Remove the bouquet garni. Set aside the oxtails and keep warm until needed. Strain the braising jus through a fine-mesh sieve lined with dampened cheesecloth. Keep warm.

To prepare the stew, cook the vegetables with bacon in a large pot until tender. Season with the salt and pepper. Add the reserved oxtails and the braising jus. For each serving, spoon a portion of the vegetables into a bowl. Arrange 2 oxtails on top. Pour some braising jus over the oxtails, and sprinkle with chopped parsley. Serve immediately.

# GRILLED VEAL RIB CHOP
## WITH TART CHERRY SAUSAGE AND PRESERVED CHERRY GLACE

SERVES 6

Veal is naturally leaner than beef, especially if it is grass fed like the veal we serve at Heartland. As such, it requires a more delicate hand in seasoning. I like to use rosemary and lavender, which complements the meat with a gentle floral note.

In mid- to late summer, the dairy farmers we buy from approach us about their veal calves. These are male calves that have been weaned and are beginning to transition to grass. The farmers can't use them because you can't milk a bull. (You can try, but I would guess the bull wouldn't be too happy.) Once the bull calves reach 150 to 175 pounds maximum weight depending upon the breed, we take them for use in the restaurant where we sell them as free-range veal. The Butternut Squash-Root Vegetable Hash is a simple variation on our popular Sweet Potato-Root Vegetable Hash (page 120).

6 veal rib chops

2 tablespoons grapeseed oil, plus additional for the sausage

1 teaspoon fine sea salt

1 teaspoon freshly ground black pepper

1 tablespoon chopped fresh rosemary

1 tablespoon teaspoon fresh lavender

6 Tart Cherry Sausages

Butternut Squash-Root Vegetable Hash

1 1/2 cups Preserved Cherry Glace de Viande

Brush the veal chops on both sides with the grapeseed oil. Season with the salt, pepper, rosemary and lavender. Set aside.

Preheat the grill to medium high. Brush the sausages with grapeseed oil and grill for about 15 minutes, until nearly cooked through. Turn and place the veal chops alongside. Grill the chops until they reach an internal temperature of 130°F for medium, and grill the sausages for 8 minutes longer, until cooked through.

To serve, place a portion of vegetable hash in the center of each plate. Slice a sausage in half diagonally and arrange on top of the hash. Prop the veal chop against the sausage. Ladle some Preserved Cherry Glace over the veal and around the edge of the hash. Serve immediately.

*(recipe continues)*

# TART CHERRY SAUSAGE

If you're tempted to try this sausage but you don't have fresh pork sausage casings on hand, go ahead and make it anyway, and form the meat mixture into patties instead of links. It's that good—and it freezes well too.

1 1/2 pounds ground veal shoulder, medium grind

3 pounds ground pork shoulder, medium grind

1 tablespoon sea salt

2 teaspoons finely ground black pepper

1 whole nutmeg, grated

2 teaspoons ground mace

2 teaspoons ground ginger

1/2 teaspoon ground cloves

1 teaspoon ground juniper berries

2 tablespoons finely chopped fresh rosemary

1 cup dried tart cherries

1 cup cold water

About 4 feet fresh pork sausage casings

Mix the veal, pork, salt, pepper, nutmeg, mace, ginger, cloves, juniper berries, rosemary, cherries and water in a large nonreactive bowl. Cover tightly with plastic wrap and refrigerate for 1 hour.

Soak fresh pork casings in cold water. Cut the casings into lengths and make a knot at one end of each casing. Using a sausage stuffer, according to manufacturer's instructions, stuff each casing with sausage mixture at a ratio of 4 sausages to 1 pound. Using kitchen string, tie off the open ends of the casings.

# BUTTERNUT SQUASH-ROOT VEGETABLE HASH

### SERVES 6

1/4 cup rendered duck fat

3/4 pound peeled, diced and blanched butternut squash or any hard winter squash

3/4 pound peeled, diced and blanched root vegetables such as turnips, parsnips and carrots

3/4 cup chopped sweet onion

1 1/2 teaspoons thyme leaves

1 1/2 teaspoons chopped Italian parsley

1 tablespoon sea salt

1 1/2 teaspoons freshly ground black pepper

Melt the fat in a large skillet over moderate heat. Add the blanched squash, root vegetables and onion and sauté until tender, 10 to 15 minutes. Using a wooden spoon to avoid breaking the vegetables, gently stir in the thyme, parsley, salt and pepper.

# PRESERVED CHERRY GLACE DE VIANDE

### MAKE 1 1/2 CUPS

Tart or sweet cherries may be used in this delicious sauce, depending on preference and availability. It keeps for one week in the refrigerator, and can be frozen for months. The glace may be reheated in small portions at the last minute and emulsified with a small knob of unsalted butter if desired.

1/2 cup dry red wine

2 cups Glace de Viande (page 270)

1/2 cup dried cherries, tart or sweet

1/2 teaspoon sea salt

1/4 teaspoon freshly ground black pepper

In a large nonreactive saucepan, heat the wine over moderate heat to a light simmer. Reduce it by half of its volume. Add the glace and simmer for 10 minutes. Add the cherries. Season with the salt and pepper.

# SMOKED BEEF SIRLOIN
## WITH MORELS AND DANDELION GREENS

In early June, when the dandelion greens are still tender and morels begin to pop up in Minnesota's woods, I like to smoke beef sirloin over last year's grapevines or a fruitwood such as cherry or apple. A honeyed brine complements the smoky flavor of the beef, while morels and piquant greens create a deliciously balanced combination.

The sirloin is located between the striploin (where you find the steak commonly referred to as New York strip) and the hind leg, where the rounds are found. It is sometimes overlooked since it is typically not as tender as the striploin, but it is chock full of flavor. This recipe celebrates that often undervalued cut.

**FOR THE BEEF**

2 quarts water

I pound light brown sugar

I cup wildflower honey

2 tablespoons chopped garlic

I cup sea salt

15 black peppercorns

5 rosemary sprigs

2 bay leaves

3 tablespoons ground cardamom

I tablespoon cayenne pepper

3 pounds beef sirloin

**FOR THE MORELS AND DANDELION GREENS**

I tablespoon unsalted butter

I teaspoon minced garlic

I teaspoon minced shallots

¼ cup cognac or brandy

12 ounces Glace de Viande (page 270)

½ pound fresh morels, cleaned

½ pound young dandelion greens, trimmed and cleaned

2 teaspoons chopped fresh rosemary

½ teaspoon sea salt

¼ teaspoon freshly ground black pepper

To prepare the brine, combine the water, sugar, honey, garlic, salt, peppercorns, rosemary, bay leaves, cardamom and cayenne in a large pot. Bring to a boil over high heat. Remove from the heat and allow the brine to cool. In a large container, pour the cooled brine over the beef sirloin, cover and refrigerate overnight.

Remove the beef from the brine, pat dry and smoke it for about 15 minutes according to the instructions for your smoker. Meanwhile, bring the brine to a gentle boil for 5 minutes, skimming occasionally. Strain the brine through a fine-mesh sieve. Baste the beef with the brine frequently while it is smoking. Cook to an internal temperature of 120°F. Allow the meat to rest for 10 minutes before slicing thinly against the grain.

While the meat is resting, prepare the morels and greens. In a large saucepan, sweat the garlic and shallots in the butter over low heat until tender, about 7 minutes. Add the cognac, increase the heat and reduce by half. Add the glace, and stir in the morels, dandelion greens and rosemary. Simmer for 30 seconds. Remove from the heat and season with salt and pepper.

To serve, arrange the smoked sliced sirloin on warm serving plates and spoon the mushrooms and greens on top.

# IOWA SNAPPING TURTLE POT-AU-FEU

Turtle is a Native American pre-European food source, still enjoyed by both indigenous and non-indigenous peoples. When I served this as part of a fixed price menu on New Year's Eve 2012, it caused quite a stir in the Twin Cities media. I acquired the turtle through a friend in Wisconsin who has a connection with a trapper in Iowa. When local food writers quizzed me about my source for turtle, I answered mysteriously, "I know a guy who knows a guy. . ." By the way, I may have taken some liberty with the title of this recipe, as it is a regional interpretation of the classic French pot-au-feu.

5 pounds turtle meat

2 cups grapeseed oil

1/2 cup vinegar

2 garlic cloves, chopped

1/2 cup all-purpose flour seasoned with 1/2 teaspoon sea salt and 1/4 teaspoon freshly ground black pepper

1/2 pound chopped bacon

1/2 cup Madeira

1/4 cup brandy or cognac

3 quarts Chicken Stock (page 267)

Bouquet garni (I sprig each basil, marjoram, sage, rosemary and thyme, plus 1/2 bay leaf, 8 black peppercorns, 8 white peppercorns, 8 coriander seeds, 3 cloves)

1/4 pound chopped carrots

1/4 pound chopped turnips

1/4 pound chopped parsnips

1/4 pound chopped onions

1/4 pound chopped leeks, white parts only

1/4 pound chopped celery

I tablespoon sea salt

2 teaspoons freshly ground black pepper

In a large nonreactive container, combine the turtle meat, oil, vinegar and garlic. Marinate for 8 hours.

Remove the turtle from the marinade and pat dry. Dust the turtle in seasoned flour. Render the bacon in a large dutch oven over moderate heat. Remove the bacon with a slotted spoon and increase the heat to moderately high. Add the turtle and brown it on all sides. Deglaze with the Madeira and brandy, making sure to scrape any bits from the bottom of the pan with a wooden spoon. Return the bacon to the pan.

*(recipe continues)*

Add the stock and bouquet garni. Cover the pan, and simmer over low heat until the turtle is very tender, 45 minutes to 1 hour. Add the carrots, turnips, parsnips, onions, leeks, celery and reserved bacon and cook until the vegetables are tender, about 20 minutes. Season with the salt and pepper. Remove the bouquet garni.

To serve, ladle into warm soup bowls and serve with a crusty baguette, or do what we did that New Year's Eve: Scoop the turtle stew into ovenproof crocks and top each one with a round of puff pastry. We gave the pastry wash of equal parts egg and whole milk, and cut a few slits in the top. Bake for about 30 minutes at 375°F.

# WILD BOAR RAGÙ
## WITH POLENTA

My former sous chef, Andy Lilja, taught me this rendition of wild boar ragú. He learned it from Filippo Caffari, a gifted chef who began his career as a butcher in Rome. It's not surprising that many of Filippo's best dishes are Italian classics featuring meat.

I have prepared this recipe using many different meats. Suffice it to say that wild boar produces the tastiest results but ground pork, beef or lamb will work too. If using lamb, substitute Marsala or madeira for the white wine, and add mint to the bouquet garni. Omit the raisins if using beef. Also, note the ingredient that makes this dish extra special: unsweetened dark chocolate. Whichever meat you use, I recommend serving the ragù over steaming, freshly cooked polenta.

⅓ cup grapeseed or extra virgin olive oil

5 pounds ground wild boar

1⅓ cups minced sweet onions

1⅓ cups minced carrots

1⅓ cups minced celery

1¼ cups white wine

3⅓ pounds fresh tomatoes, roasted and pureed (or substitute canned, peeled and strained tomatoes)

Bouquet garni (1 garlic bulb, 1 rosemary sprig, 10 thyme sprigs, 5 oregano sprigs, 1 parsley bunch, 1 nutmeg, 4 allspice, 15 black peppercorns)

½ cinnamon stick

1 cup golden raisins

⅓ cup grated unsweetened dark chocolate

1 tablespoon fine sea salt

1 teaspoon freshly ground black pepper

Basic Polenta (page 92)

In a large nonreactive pot, warm the oil over moderate heat. Add the boar and cook until brown, stirring to break up the meat. Add the onions, carrots and celery and cook for 10 minutes longer. Pour in the wine and reduce by half. Add the tomatoes and bouquet garni and continue to cook, reducing the ragù by half again. Simmer for 1½ hours.

Add the cinnamon stick to the ragù. Add some water if the ragù becomes too thick. Simmer for 30 minutes longer.

Remove the bouquet garni and cinnamon stick. Stir in the raisins, chocolate, salt and pepper until the chocolate is fully melted. If not serving immediately, transfer to a container and chill in an ice bath before refrigerating.

# ELK ROAST

### WITH BLACKBERRY GLACE AND TOASTED WALNUT WILD RICE

SERVES 12 TO 14

At one time, Minnesota's native elk were abundant, roaming a range that traversed the entire state up to caribou country in the far northeast. As settlement and over-hunting pushed the herds northward and their habitat disappeared, elk nearly became extinct in these parts.

Conservation efforts in 1913 helped reestablish elk, with a good portion of the animals coming from a farm right here in Ramsey County. In addition to modest-sized herds in northern and central Minnesota, elk are being farmed in relative abundance in neighboring Wisconsin too. For those unfamiliar with elk, they belong to the deer family and are one of largest land mammals in North America, second only to the moose.

| | |
|---|---|
| 7 pound elk roast, trimmed and trussed | 2 cups whole blackberries, puréed and strained |
| 2 tablespoons sea salt | I teaspoon unsalted butter |
| 2 tablespoons freshly ground black pepper | 2 teaspoons sea salt |
| 4 tablespoons chopped fresh rosemary | I teaspoon freshly ground black pepper |
| 3 tablespoons rendered duck fat or unsalted butter | Handful of fresh blackberries, for garnish |
| 5 cups Glace de Viande (page 270) | Toasted Walnut Wild Rice |

Preheat the oven to 375°F. Season the elk with salt, pepper and rosemary. Melt the duck fat in a large skillet over moderately high heat and add the elk. Sear until well browned on all sides. Place the elk on a roasting rack set inside a large, foil-lined sheet pan. Roast to an internal temperature of 110°. Remove the elk from the oven, and let it rest for 10 minutes before slicing very thinly on the diagonal.

In a nonreactive saucepan, warm the glace over moderate heat until barely simmering. Stir in the blackberry purée. Remove the pan from the heat and whisk in the butter. Season with salt and pepper. Before serving, add the fresh blackberries to the warm sauce. To serve, ladle sauce on warm plates, spoon the wild rice on one side, and arrange the sliced elk on top. Serve immediately.

# TOASTED WALNUT WILD RICE

SERVES 10 TO 12

In Minnesota, wild rice is held in high esteem. This savory pilaf is the perfect side dish for almost any grilled or roasted meat. You will know the rice is properly cooked when the kernels crack and the grain just becomes fluffy.

2 quarts Chicken Stock (page 267)

3 cups wild rice, well rinsed

I cup chopped bacon

1 1/2 teaspoons unsalted butter

I cup mirepoix (finely chopped carrot, celery and onion)

1/2 cup sherry

1 1/2 teaspoons fine sea salt

1/2 teaspoon freshly ground black pepper

2 tablespoons chopped fresh rosemary

2 cups toasted walnuts

In a nonreactive pot, bring the chicken stock to boil. Add the wild rice and reduce heat to a simmer. Cover and cook until the wild rice is tender, about 45 minutes. Drain and transfer the rice to two large sheet pans, spreading it out evenly with a spatula to cool.

Return the pot to moderate heat and cook the bacon until the fat is rendered. Add the butter. When the butter begins to foam, add the chopped carrot, celery and onion. Cook until tender. Deglaze the pan with the sherry. Add the cooked wild rice and reduce the heat to low. Stir in the salt, pepper, rosemary and walnuts.

# GRILLED BISON TENDERLOIN
## WITH PUMPKIN SEED PISTOU

North American bison were once so numerous they were called "thunder of the plains." Now, aside from a few rejuvenated wild herds on federal and state parkland, bison are primarily free ranged on farmland as an agricultural commodity. It is a glorious experience to see these majestic native bovine animals up close. We serve their delicious meat with Wheat Berry-Preserved Cherry Salad and my Heartland interpretation of a classic green sauce or pistou, made with local pumpkin seeds. Bison is best served medium rare; it's leaner than beef tenderloin, which we cook to 120°F.

6 bison tenderloin filets
(5 ounces each)

3 tablespoons grapeseed oil

I tablespoon sea salt

3/4 teaspoon freshly ground
black pepper

2 1/2 tablespoons chopped rosemary

Wheat Berry-Preserved Cherry Salad

6 tablespoons Pumpkin Seed Parsley
Pistou (page 264)

Preheat the grill to medium. Brush the bison on both sides with the grapeseed oil and season with salt, pepper and rosemary. Grill the bison to an internal temperature of 120°F for medium rare, about 4 minutes per side. Allow to rest for 10 minutes before slicing thinly.

To serve, divide the Wheat Berry-Preserved Cherry Salad among warm plates and arrange slices of bison filet alongside. Top with a spoonful of Pumpkin Seed Parsley Pistou.

*(recipe continues)*

# WHEAT BERRY–PRESERVED CHERRY SALAD

Wheat berries, or whole-grain wheat kernels, are tender yet pleasantly chewy when cooked properly.

1 cup dried wheat berries

2 tablespoons green onions, sliced on the bias

2 tablespoons dried cherries

1/2 teaspoon chopped fresh mint

1 tablespoon apple cider vinegar

1 teaspoon fine sea salt

1 tablespoon grapeseed oil

1 1/2 tablespoons walnut oil

1/4 teaspoon freshly ground black pepper

To cook the wheat berries, combine with two cups water in a medium saucepan. Bring to a boil over moderately high heat, then reduce to a simmer. Cover and cook for about 45 minutes or until the wheat berries are fully cooked and tender. Check the berries every 15 minutes while cooking, and add more water if necessary. Drain if necessary.

Combine the wheat berries, onions, cherries and mint in a nonreactive bowl. Whisk together the vinegar and salt, then whisk in the oils and pepper. Gently mix into the wheat berries.

# VENISON PORTERHOUSE CHOP
## WITH PLUMS, ZINFANDEL AND ROSEMARY

Venison chops are a nice alternative to the steak or pork chop you might serve at a backyard barbecue. We get our venison from Judith and Larry Gergen of Burr Oaks Red Deer Farm in the aptly named town of Fertile, Iowa. Red deer, native to Europe, are the preferred species for ranchers. Our native whitetail deer do not domesticate well, nor do they produce the optimum meat-to-bone ratio that would make them a profitable pursuit.

6 venison porterhouse chops,
8 to 10 ounces each

6 fresh plums, halved and pitted

4 tablespoons grapeseed oil

1 teaspoon sea salt

1 teaspoon freshly ground
black pepper

1 tablespoon unsalted butter, divided

1 tablespoon minced garlic

2 teaspoons minced shallots

3/4 cup zinfandel

3/4 cup ruby port

1 1/2 cups Glace de Viande (page 270)

1 tablespoon chopped fresh rosemary

6 ounces Stone Fruit Catsup
(page 254)

Brush the venison chops on both sides, and the cut side of the plums, with grapeseed oil. Season the chops and plums with salt and pepper. Set aside.

Meanwhile, melt half the butter in a medium saucepan over moderate heat. Reduce heat and add the garlic and shallots. Sweat until tender. Add the zinfandel and port. Increase the heat and reduce the wines by half. Add the glace and rosemary. Simmer for 1 minute. Stir in the catsup. Remove from heat, whisk in the remaining butter and set aside.

Preheat a grill to medium. Grill the chops for 3 minutes per side. Score the cut side of the plums, and place them cut side down on the grill for about 3 minutes. Be careful not to overcook the plums; they should be warmed through but not falling apart.

To serve, spoon the sauce on six plates. Place the chops on top and garnish with two plum halves. Serve immediately.

# HUNTER-STYLE RABBIT

Like many of Italian descent, I grew up eating rabbit. My great-uncle had a shop in Hoboken where he sold fresh rabbits slaughtered and cleaned to order. In the Midwest, eating rabbit is a hunter's tradition. Years ago, this was never an issue. But in this age of internet access and anonymous trolling critics, my proclivity for cooking with rabbit has occasionally posed challenges. I am referring to animal rights activists who read my menus online and mistake the farm-raised rabbits I serve for the floppy-eared kind people keep as pets.

The average weight of a rabbit is about three and a half pounds. The hind legs weigh 8 to 10 ounces each once the bones have been removed.

| | |
|---|---|
| 6 rabbit legs, thigh and hip bone removed (3 1/2 pounds total) | 3/4 pound chopped carrot |
| 2 teaspoons sea salt | 3/4 pound chopped sweet onions |
| 1 teaspoon freshly ground black pepper | 12 garlic cloves, peeled |
| 1 tablespoon chopped fresh rosemary | 3/4 pound wild mushrooms, cleaned and trimmed |
| 2 tablespoons rendered duck fat | 3/4 cup brandy |
| 6 ounces chopped bacon | 3 cups Glace de Viande (page 270) |
| | 1 tablespoon unsalted butter |

Season the rabbit on both sides with salt and pepper and sprinkle with the rosemary. In a large skillet, sear the rabbit in the duck fat over moderately high heat, then reduce the heat to low and continue to pan roast uncovered until just barely cooked through. It is very important that the rabbit not be overcooked, or it will become dry. Remove from the pan and set aside.

Return the pan to moderate heat and add the bacon, carrots, onions and garlic, stirring occasionally, until the vegetables are tender. (Add a bit of butter if the pan seems dry.) Add the mushrooms, and deglaze with the brandy. Add the meat glace. Heat until the sauce begins to thicken. Turn off the heat. Whisk in the butter and season the sauce with the salt and pepper. Return the rabbit to the pan, and spoon some of the sauce over the top.

For each serving, spoon a portion of the vegetables and sauce into a serving bowl, place the rabbit on it and top with more sauce. Make sure the rabbit is positioned in the bowl with the leg bone up.

# POULTRY
*and*
# GAME BIRDS

One of my challenges is to
understand Minnesota's traditions,
reinterpreting recipes that hunters
feasted on at the family table, and
then adding a few of my own.

# POULTRY
*and*
# GAME BIRDS

ROASTED CHICKEN BREAST
with Braised Greens and Carrot-Fennel Broth• 191

STEWED CHICKEN
with Cider Cream Sauce and Root Vegetables • 194

COQ AU VIN • 195

MIDWESTERN CASSOULET • 197

DUCK BREAST
with Lobster Mushrooms • 202

PAN ROASTED SQUAB with Peaches • 203

GOOSE BREAST
with Early Apples and Roasted Garlic • 207

GRILLED MARINATED QUAIL
with Watercress and Pickled Shiitakes • 208

FREE RANGE TURKEY-WILD MUSHROOM STEW • 211

# ROASTED CHICKEN BREAST
## WITH BRAISED GREENS AND CARROT-FENNEL BROTH

No one moves to Minnesota for the weather. We're known for extreme swings in temperature, and I don't just mean from season to season. This recipe was created with Minnesota's summer heat in mind. Not only does it employ a pure, simple broth of carrot and fennel juices, but it also showcases the midsummer greens that farmers end up harvesting all at once when temperatures begin to climb, lest the greens bolt and become unusable. We communicate regularly with our farmers so we can be ready to create menus that incorporate as much of those greens as possible.

At Heartland, we prepare the boneless, skin-on chicken breast with an "airline" cut, the wing still attached. If you're handy with cutting chicken, try it, for it creates an attractive presentation. Otherwise, boneless chicken breasts will serve you well. I've specified duck fat over butter or oil for cooking both chicken and greens. The fat from pasture-raised ducks is more healthful than butter, since it's higher in beneficial fatty acids. You also don't need as much; a little duck fat goes a long way, and makes everything taste a little better.

| | |
|---|---|
| 5 pounds carrots | 6 boneless chicken breast halves, skin on (about 2 1/2 pounds) |
| 1 pound fennel bulbs, quartered | |
| Bouquet garni (1 teaspoon fennel seeds, 3 tarragon sprigs, 3 parsley sprigs, 1 bay leaf) | 1 teaspoon sea salt |
| | 1 teaspoon freshly ground black pepper |
| 1 teaspoon sea salt | 1 tablespoon rendered duck fat |
| 1/2 teaspoon freshly ground white pepper | Braised Greens |

To make the broth, pass the carrots and fennel through a vegetable juicer. Transfer the juice to a nonreactive saucepan and add the bouquet garni. Bring to a simmer over moderately high heat, skimming any pulp from the surface with a spoon. Do not let it boil. When the broth is completely clear, after about 5 minutes, strain it through a fine-mesh sieve lined with dampened cheesecloth. Discard the bouquet garni. Add the salt and pepper.

Preheat the oven to 375°. Season the chicken with salt and pepper. Melt the fat in an ovenproof skillet or dutch oven over moderately high heat and add the chicken skin side down. Sear for about 5 minutes, until the skin has begun to brown. Transfer the pan to the oven and roast until the chicken is fully cooked, about 15 minutes.

To serve, place a portion of braised greens on each plate and top with a chicken breast and 1/4 cup of the carrot-fennel broth.

## BRAISED GREENS

SERVES 6

I call for spinach or chard, but this recipe also works nicely with beet greens, turnip greens and collards. Cooking time varies depending on the greens you choose; beet greens and collards take the longest. Serve the braised greens beneath fish or chicken, or as an accompaniment to roasted meats.

4 tablespoons rendered duck fat or unsalted butter

4 tablespoons chopped garlic

2 pounds fresh greens such as spinach and chard, trimmed

I cup Court-Bouillon (page 268) or vegetable broth

2 teaspoons sea salt

I teaspoon freshly ground black pepper

I teaspoon grated nutmeg

Melt the fat in a large, nonreactive skillet over moderate heat. Add the garlic and greens. Stir until the greens begin to wilt. Add the court-bouillon. Stir in the salt, pepper and nutmeg. Continue cooking until the court-bouillon is nearly evaporated.

# STEWED CHICKEN
## WITH CIDER CREAM SAUCE AND ROOT VEGETABLES

Here's a comforting dish composed of those excess chicken legs and thighs that seem to accumulate in our walk-in. I originally developed the recipe for rabbit, and think it is even better that way. If you have access to fresh rabbits, try substituting a channel-boned hind leg (with thigh and hip bones removed) for the chicken thigh and leg. The rabbit will cook more quickly and evenly, and be easier for your guests to enjoy.

6 free range chicken thighs, about 1¼ pounds

6 free range chicken legs, about 2 pounds

Seasoned all-purpose flour

4 tablespoons butter

4 cups apple cider

Bouquet garni (1 rosemary sprig, 1 bay leaf, 6 black peppercorns and 1 whole nutmeg)

4 cups Chicken Stock (page 267)

1 teaspoon sea salt

½ teaspoon freshly ground black pepper

½ cup heavy cream

1 tablespoon chopped Italian parsley

1½ pounds root vegetables (carrots, turnips, parsnips and rutabagas), peeled and diced

1½ teaspoons sea salt

¾ teaspoon freshly ground white pepper

Dust the chicken with seasoned flour. Melt 2 tablespoons of the butter in a skillet or Dutch oven over moderate heat. Add half the chicken skin side down. Brown on both sides and remove to a plate. Repeat with remaining chicken.

Pour the apple cider into the pan and bring to a boil, then reduce to a simmer, scraping any bits from the bottom of the pan with a wooden spoon. Add the bouquet garni and chicken stock. Return the chicken to the pan.

Cover and simmer over low heat until the chicken is very tender, 45 minutes to an hour. Remove the bouquet garni and season with salt and pepper. Add the cream and parsley.

In a large skillet, melt the remaining 2 tablespoon of butter. Add the root vegetables and sauté over moderate heat until tender but not browned, about 10 minutes. Season to taste with salt and white pepper. To serve, spoon the vegetables into shallow serving bowls. Arrange the chicken on top. Pour the sauce over the chicken and serve immediately.

# COQ AU VIN

SERVES 6

We go through a lot of whole, free-range chickens at the restaurant, and I am always searching for ways to use the legs and thighs. Sometimes they end up in sausage or in a small plate to serve in our lounge. But other times, they inspire my version of a classic French bistro dish. Substitute dry white wine for the red, and you'll have coq au vin blanc.

6 chicken thighs, about 1¼ pounds

6 chicken legs, about 2 pounds

1 bottle (750 ml) dry red wine

Seasoned all-purpose flour

¼ pound slab bacon, finely diced

3 carrots, peeled and diced

3 potatoes, peeled and diced

3 turnips, peeled and diced

¼ pound pearl onions, peeled

12 crimini or button mushrooms, quartered

12 garlic cloves

1 tablespoon butter

¼ cup cognac or brandy

Bouquet garni (1 Italian parsley sprig, 1 thyme sprig, 1 marjoram sprig, 1 bay leaf, 12 black peppercorns, 6 white peppercorns, 1 whole nutmeg)

1 teaspoon sea salt

½ teaspoon freshly ground black pepper

1 cup fresh bread crumbs

1 tablespoon chopped Italian parsley

Place the chicken in a deep nonreactive bowl. Pour in the wine, making sure to completely cover most of the chicken. Cover and refrigerate overnight.

Remove the chicken from the bowl, reserving the wine. Dust the chicken in seasoned flour. In a braising pan over moderate heat, cook the bacon until brown, about 10 minutes. Add the carrots, potatoes, turnips, onions, mushrooms and garlic and cook until lightly browned. Remove the bacon and vegetables and set aside.

Melt the butter in the pan and add the chicken. Cook over moderately high heat until browned on both sides. Add the red wine and cognac, scraping bits from the bottom of the pan with a wooden spoon. Add the bouquet garni. Cover the pan and simmer over low heat until the chicken is very tender, about 1 hour.

Preheat the oven to 350°F. Return the vegetables to the pan. Season with the salt and pepper and simmer for 15 minutes. Transfer the coq au vin to a ceramic or glass baking dish. Sprinkle the bread crumbs on top, and place in the oven until the stew begins to bubble and the bread crumbs have browned, about 15 minutes. Remove from the oven and garnish with chopped parsley. Serve immediately.

# MIDWESTERN CASSOULET

A chef from a small town in southwestern France taught me this recipe. Cassoulet has many versions, and this is somewhat typical of what might be served in Toulouse. I have adapted it over the years with ingredients readily available here in Minnesota.

The composition of the ragoût depends on what we have in the way of shoulder cuts or other parts that are best when stewed after butchering. I have used a combination of pork, beef and lamb—or bison, goat and wild boar. The basic cassoulet keeps for a week or two in the refrigerator and also freezes well. You'll be happy to have the leftovers.

½ cup rendered duck fat (rendered pork fat or unsalted butter may be substituted)

2 pounds sweet onions, peeled and diced

10 garlic cloves

4 pounds diced lean pork

2 pounds white wine garlic sausage (or another French-style pork sausage), cooked and sliced on the bias

1 pound Great Northern Beans, cooked (page 200)

2 quarts Chicken Stock (page 267)

2 cups reserved bean cooking liquid

4 Roma tomatoes or 2 large ripe tomatoes, seeded and chopped

2 tablespoons tomato concentrate

1 bouquet garni (2 parsley sprigs, 2 thyme sprigs, 1 bay leaf, 1 whole nutmeg)

1 tablespoon sea salt

½ tablespoon freshly ground black pepper

Fresh bread crumbs and rendered fat or unsalted butter for serving

10 to 12 legs Duck Confit (page 201)

In a large dutch oven, melt the duck fat and add the onions and garlic. Cook over moderately high heat for 5 minutes, until softened but not browned. Add the pork and sausage and cook for 10 minutes, until the pork is well browned. Add the beans, stock and reserved cooking liquid. When the ragoût begins to simmer, stir in the tomatoes and tomato concentrate. Add the bouquet garni, and season the ragoût with the salt and pepper. Cover the pan and simmer for 1 hour. If not using the ragout immediately, chill in an ice water bath before refrigerating or freezing.

To serve, preheat the oven to 400°. Divide the ragoût among ovenproof baking crocks. Top generously with fresh bread crumbs, and dot with small knobs of rendered

*(recipe continues)*

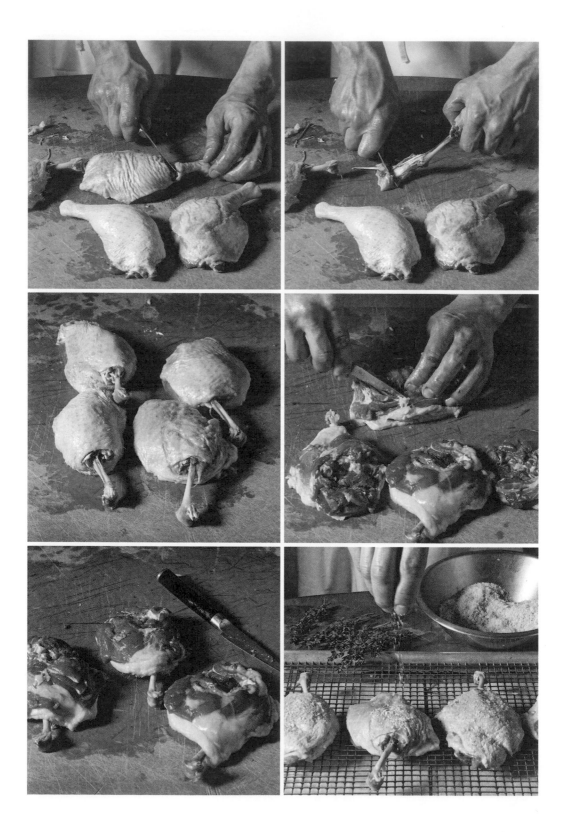

fat or butter. Place a leg of duck confit on top of the beans. Place on baking sheets and bake until the cassoulet begins to bubble and the bread crumbs are nicely browned, 15 to 20 minutes. Remove and serve immediately.

## GREAT NORTHERN BEANS

SERVES 10 TO 12

I pound Great Northern beans, rinsed and checked for stones

I smoked pork hock (or subtitute 1/2 pound diced smoked bacon)

I sweet onion, peeled and studded with cloves

I large carrot, peeled

Bouquet garni (2 parsley sprigs, 2 thyme sprigs, I bay leaf, 2 garlic cloves, 15 black peppercorns)

To prepare the beans, soak them overnight in twice their volume of water. Drain the beans, and combine in a large pot with the pork hocks, onion, carrot and bouquet garni. Pour in enough cold water to cover by twice the volume of beans. Bring to a boil over high heat. Reduce to a simmer, and gently cook until the beans are tender but not splitting, about 1 1/2 hours. Add more water as needed to maintain a soupy consistency.

Drain the beans, reserving the cooking liquid. Remove the onion, carrot and the bouquet garni. Turn the beans out onto sheet pans and allow them to cool. Pull the meat off the pork hock and add to the beans, discarding the bones.

# DUCK CONFIT

SERVES 6 TO 8

We begin stockpiling duck leg confit in late summer and early autumn, to give it enough time to cure in its catacomb of fat before winter arrives. That's when cassoulet begins to appear on Heartland's menus.

This recipe is a classic approach to preserving meat harvested during hunting season. It's very straightforward, as you'll see in the step-by-step instructions on pages 198-199. The basic formula is easily adapted to other birds such as turkey, goose and pheasant, as well as to meats including boneless lamb shoulder, boneless pork shoulder and rabbit. If we run low on duck confit, we may even substitute pork belly that has been braised, pressed and caramelized in a hot skillet.

| | |
|---|---|
| 5 pounds duck legs, thigh bone and leg joint removed | ¹/2 teaspoon cayenne pepper |
| 2 tablespoons sea salt | 1 handful thyme sprigs |
| | 5 cups rendered duck fat |

Toss the duck legs in the salt and cayenne until well coated. Arrange skin side up on a roasting rack inside a large foil-lined pan. Place a couple of sprigs of thyme on top of each leg. Refrigerate the legs uncovered overnight.

Preheat the oven to 200° F.

Transfer the duck legs to a deep roasting pan. Heat the duck fat in a nonreactive pot until liquid (160° F.). Pour the liquid fat over the duck legs, making sure they are completely submerged. This is very important because the finished confit must not come into contact with air until it is ready to be used. Cover the pan tightly with foil, place in the oven and cook slowly for a minimum of 6 hours, until the legs are very tender but not falling apart. Do not remove the foil.

Refrigerate the duck legs until the fat hardens. Check to make sure that an airtight seal has been created by the hardened fat. The confit can be kept undisturbed for up to 6 months. To retrieve the confit, heat the pan in a slow oven to 160° F. until the fat liquefies. Do not allow the duck to cook. Remove from the liquid fat, and use within 7 days.

# DUCK BREAST
## WITH LOBSTER MUSHROOMS

In a brief, shining window of time between golden chanterelle and hen-of-the-woods seasons, we see lobster mushrooms, named for their deep orange color. In Minnesota, they appear in late summer, around the same time as the first early apples such as Prairie Spy and Sweet Sixteen.

Found scattered throughout pine and aspen woods, lobster mushrooms are actually one of two different varieties of fungus (*Russula brevipes* or *Lactarius piperatus*), which are parasitized by a mold called *Hypomyces lactifluorum*. This mold covers the mushrooms with a distinctive orange skin and transforms them into choice wild edibles. We find the *Russula* variety and sometimes the spicier *Lactarius* too.

6 boneless duck breasts

6 tablespoons cognac or brandy

3/4 cup hard apple cider

1 teaspoon minced garlic

1 teaspoon minced shallots

6 ounces lobster mushrooms, sliced

1 1/2 cups Glace de Viande (page 270)

1 teaspoon chopped fresh tarragon

1 tablespoon unsalted butter

1/2 teaspoon sea salt

1/4 teaspoon freshly ground black pepper

1 early-season red apple, cored and sliced

Score the duck breasts in a cross-hatch pattern on the skin side, taking care not to cut into the meat. Season on both sides with salt and pepper.

Heat a large skillet over moderate heat, and place the duck, skin side down, in the pan. Slowly render the fat until the skin is crisp. Lower the heat if necessary to ensure that the skin is nicely browned but not burnt. Drain the fat from the pan, leaving about a tablespoon behind. (The drained fat may be reserved for future use, such as frying potatoes.) Increase the heat to moderately high, and flip the duck breasts. Sear the duck, flesh side down, until nicely browned, 2 to 3 minutes.

Remove the duck from the pan and allow it to rest. Deglaze the pan with the cognac and add the cider. Reduce the liquid by half. Add the garlic, shallots and mushrooms. Reduce the heat to a simmer. Cook for 2 minutes before adding the glace and tarragon. Remove from the heat and whisk in the butter. Season with the salt and pepper. Stir in the apples. To serve, slice each breast on a radical bias and fan out among 6 plates. Spoon the sauce over the duck. Serve immediately.

# PAN-ROASTED SQUAB
## WITH PEACHES

A few years back, Minnesota reopened dove hunting season, which had been closed for generations due to overhunting. Since the dove population had rebounded, it seemed both acceptable and prudent to allow hunting again.

The folks at Minnesota Public Radio, who know they can count on me for a lively quote no matter how controversial, and who also know that squab sometimes graces my menus, called me for an interview to be broadcast on their affiliate stations. Callers were objecting to the fact that doves, a symbol of peace, were being blasted out of the sky by hunters wielding shotguns. I don't remember exactly what I said, but it was something about doves being tasty and let us not confuse a symbol with an actual bird. Just because Donald Duck talks doesn't mean that your duck confit once expressed an opinion.

A squab is a baby pigeon or dove, prized for its succulence and depth of flavor—in other words, a nestling. I can't call them baby pigeons since customers will not eat anything described with the word "baby' that previously had a beating heart. Hence the terms "veal" for baby cow, "lamb" for baby sheep and "poussin" instead of baby chicken.

| | |
|---|---|
| 12 peaches (preferably a white freestone variety) | 3 garlic cloves |
| 6 squabs (dove or pigeon), dressed | 3 tablespoons cognac |
| Salt and pepper | 3 tablespoons Grand Marnier |
| 6 tablespoons unsalted butter | 3 cups Chicken Stock (page 267) |
| 1½ tablespoons grapeseed oil | Bouquet garni (15 black peppercorns, 3 thyme sprigs, 3 bay leaves, 1 slice fresh ginger) |
| 3 shallots, peeled | |
| | 1½ teaspoons superfine sugar |

Bring a saucepan of water to a boil. Cut a small X on the bottom of each peach and plunge into boiling water for 10 seconds. Transfer to an ice water bath to cool. Peel the peaches and cut in half lengthwise to remove the stones. Be careful not to damage the peach halves. Reserve 12 peach halves, and set aside the skins and stones along with the remaining peach halves for the sauce.

*(recipe continues)*

Preheat the oven to 450°F. Season the squab inside and outside with salt and pepper and brush with 3 tablespoons melted butter. Heat the oil in a large ovenproof skillet over high heat and lightly brown the squabs on all sides. Place in the oven and roast for 12 minutes. Remove the squab to a cutting board and let it rest for 10 minutes before removing the breast meat from the bones. Reserve the bones.

To make the sauce, pour off and discard most of the fat from the pan and place over high heat. Add 1½ tablespoons of butter, the shallots, garlic, squab bones, reserved peach skins and stones and the remaining peach halves. Deglaze the pan with the cognac and Grand Marnier, using a wooden spoon to scrape any bits from the bottom of the pan. Reduce the liquid by two thirds. Add the stock and bouquet garni. Simmer over gentle heat for 20 minutes, occasionally skimming the surface of fat and impurities. Strain the sauce through a fine-mesh sieve, return it to the pan and reduce until it becomes slightly syrupy. Add 1½ tablespoons of butter and season with salt and pepper to taste.

Preheat the broiler. Place the reserved peach halves on a baking sheet, cut side up, and sprinkle with the sugar. Broil for 2 to 3 minutes, until lightly caramelized. For each serving, slice and fan a peach half on a plate. Top with a pair of squab breasts and place the other peach half at the top. Spoon some of the sauce over the squabs and serve with roasted potatoes and leeks.

# GOOSE BREAST
WITH EARLY APPLES AND ROASTED GARLIC

This harvest-season recipe celebrates the glorious goose, pairing apples and the unexpected twist of cocoa powder, which adds richness and an interesting bitter note that balances the apples' sweetness. Make sure to use a high quality unsweetened cocoa powder, and a sweet early apple. In Minnesota, that means Haralson or Regent.

3 boneless goose breasts, halved (about 5 pounds total)

Salt and pepper

2 ounces cognac or brandy

1/3 cup unfiltered apple cider

3 teaspoons puréed roasted garlic

3 teaspoons minced shallots

1 cup Glace de Viande (page 270)

2 teaspoons chopped rosemary

1 teaspoon cocoa powder

1 tablespoon unsalted butter

3 medium red apples, cored and thinly sliced

Score the goose breasts in a cross-hatch pattern on the skin side, taking care not to cut the meat. Season on both sides with salt and pepper. Heat a large skillet over moderate heat and place the goose, skin side down, in the pan. Slowly render the fat until the skin is crisp, reducing the heat if necessary to ensure that the skin is nicely browned but not burnt. Drain the fat from the pan, leaving about a tablespoon behind. (The drained fat may be reserved for future use, including stellar fried potatoes.)

Increase the heat to moderately high, and flip the goose breasts. Sear the goose, flesh side down, until nicely browned, about 3 minutes. Remove the goose from the pan and allow it to rest. Deglaze the pan with the cognac, and add the apple cider. Reduce the liquid by half. Add the roasted garlic purée and shallots. Reduce the heat to a simmer and cook for 2 minutes before adding the glace and rosemary. Remove the pan from the heat and whisk in the cocoa followed by the butter. Season with the salt and pepper.

To serve, fan 6 apple slices on each serving plate. Slice the goose on a radical bias and fan it out, opposite the apples. Spoon the sauce on top.

# GRILLED MARINATED QUAIL
## WITH WATERCRESS AND PICKLED SHIITAKES

Some of the best dishes I created at the now-defunct Loring Café were born out of sheer necessity when the farmers I bought from found themselves with more produce than they could sell. Since we changed the menu daily, they knew they could count on me to create something that would use their bumper crops. This dish was conceived one evening when faced with an abundance of baby greens straight from the farm, and a passel of shiitake mushrooms. I like to grill the quail so it remains slightly pink inside, but it can also be fried in butter or rendered duck fat and then finished in the oven.

If so inclined, try garnishing this dish as I do, with a small amount of Crisp Leeks. To make them, simply clean and finely julienne the white part of a young leek. Fry the leek julienne in a small saucepan of grapeseed oil or canola oil heated to 350°F until lightly browned, and drain on paper towels. Be sure to salt the leeks when they are still warm since the heat helps the salt to adhere.

| | |
|---|---|
| I tablespoon sea salt | 6 semi-boneless quail |
| 1/2 cup dry white wine | 12 ounces watercress or mixed seasonal greens, cleaned and trimmed |
| I cup grapeseed oil | |
| 2 tablespoons thyme leaves | 1 1/2 cup Shiitake Mushroom Vinaigrette |
| I tablespoon minced garlic | |
| I teaspoon freshly ground white pepper | 24 Pickled Shiitakes |
| | Crisp leeks (optional) |

In a large nonreactive bowl, dissolve the salt in the wine. Whisk in the oil, thyme, garlic and pepper. Add the quail and mix with your hands to combine with the marinade. Cover tightly with plastic wrap and refrigerate for at least 2 hours.

Preheat a grill. Grill the quails to medium doneness. Set aside. Meanwhile, toss the greens in the vinaigrette, and divide among six chilled serving plates. Arrange the quails and pickled shiitakes on top of the greens. Top with the crisp leeks, if desired.

*(recipe continues)*

# SHIITAKE MUSHROOM VINAIGRETTE

MAKES 2¼ CUPS

1 teaspoon sea salt

¼ cup champagne vinegar

½ cup Mushroom Broth (page 274) or vegetable stock

1½ cups grapeseed oil

1 tablespoon minced garlic

½ tablespoon minced shallots

1 tablespoon thyme leaves

1 teaspoon freshly ground white pepper

6 shiitake mushroom caps, blanched and thinly sliced

In a medium bowl, dissolve the salt in the vinegar. Whisk in the mushroom broth, oil, garlic, shallots, thyme, pepper and shiitakes. Refrigerate until ready to use.

# PICKLED SHIITAKES

SERVES 8 TO 10

Be sure to ventilate your kitchen when preparing this savory accompaniment. If you have never inhaled simmering vinegar, I don't suggest you start now.

1 pound cleaned shiitake mushrooms, caps only

1 cup champagne vinegar

½ cup granulated sugar

1 teaspoon sea salt

½ teaspoon freshly ground white pepper

2 tablespoon chopped fresh rosemary

1 tablespoon minced garlic

1 tablespoons minced shallots

Place the mushrooms in a heatproof container. In a nonreactive saucepan, heat the vinegar, sugar, salt, pepper, rosemary, garlic and shallots over high heat until the mixture just begins to boil. Remove from the heat and pour the marinade over the mushrooms. Allow them to cool, then cover tightly. Refrigerate overnight or until needed.

# FREE RANGE TURKEY–WILD MUSHROOM STEW

Wherever I go in Minnesota, I see wild turkeys roaming freely. I've seen them in downtown St. Paul and downtown Minneapolis. They come up from the Mississippi River Valley, and they seem to have no fear. They probably know that discharging a firearm within city limits is against the law, so they go about shaking their tail feathers in defiance. While they appear to be oblivious, they are, in fact, extremely wily. Just ask any hunter.

Since wild turkeys are hard to come by in most places, I have adapted this for a domestic bird. It calls for roasting a whole 10-to 12-pound free range turkey, so if you decide to make it you might want to invite several friends to enjoy it with you. It's a good dish to adapt in smaller quantity for leftover Thanksgiving turkey.

| | |
|---|---|
| 10 to 12-pound free range turkey, roasted and boned | 1/4 cup chopped fresh rosemary |
| 1 pound slab bacon, diced | 1 tablespoon butter or duck fat, optional |
| 1 pound carrots, peeled and diced | 1/2 cup brandy |
| 1 pound sweet onion, diced | 4 quarts Brown Veal Stock (page 269) or beef stock |
| 1 pounds chopped celery | 11/2 tablespoons sea salt |
| 10 garlic cloves | 1 tablespoon freshly ground black pepper |
| 21/2 pounds assorted wild mushrooms, cleaned and trimmed | |

Pull and dice the turkey into 1/2-inch pieces, discarding skin and fat.

In a large dutch oven, cook the diced bacon until the fat is rendered. Add the carrots, onions, celery, garlic, mushrooms and rosemary and sauté until tender, about 8 minutes. Add a small amount of butter or duck fat if necessary. Deglaze with the brandy.

Add the glace or stock to the pan. Cook over moderately high heat until the sauce begins to thicken. Add the turkey, and season with the salt and pepper. Break out the crusty bread and enjoy.

# DESSERTS
*and*
# TREATS

In local legend, Paul Bunyan ate
such big flapjacks that it took 50 men
with pork rinds tied to their feet
to grease the griddle.

# DESSERTS
*and*
# TREATS

SORGHUM CUSTARD CHOCOLATE TART • 215

PUMPKIN KUCHEN • 218

SUMMER CORN POTS DE CRÈME • 219

RASPBERRY PECAN LINZER TORTE • 222

WILD RICE MADELEINES • 227

CRANBERRY SHORTCAKE • 228

CHOCOLATE MAPLE ROULADE • 231

CHESTNUT PANNA COTTA with Honey Oat Tuiles • 233

HONEY POACHED PLUMS with Candied Pecans • 237

PUMPKIN SEED FRANGIPANE TART with Brandied Prunes • 238

HONEY GOAT CHEESE GATEAUX with Red Currant Coulis • 240

CORNMEAL MARSALA-RAISIN BISCOTTI • 243

CLASSIC BUTTERMILK FLAPJACKS • 244

BUTTERMILK BISCUITS • 246

SPICY OATMEAL CRACKERS • 247

WILD RICE CRACKERS • 248

# SORGHUM CUSTARD CHOCOLATE TART

In the Heartland kitchen, we regularly use sorghum syrup as an alternative sweetener. We buy it through a cooperative called the Southeast Minnesota Food Network, a great local source for ingredients produced by small farmers, many of them Amish. Sorghum has a very pronounced flavor, and it gives this tart a unique and pleasant edge. Barley malt syrup is a good alternative. The chocolate short dough tart shell provides a nice complement to the sorghum. The recipe makes enough for four shells, but it takes just as long to make one as it does to make four, and it's nice to have frozen tart dough on hand for impromptu fruit pies.

| | |
|---|---|
| I cup brown sugar | 2 tablespoons unsalted butter, melted |
| 2 large eggs | 1/4 cup sorghum syrup |
| 3 egg yolks | |
| 2 tablespoons heavy cream | Chocolate Short Dough tart shell |

Preheat the oven to 350°F. To prepare the filling, whisk together the brown sugar, eggs, egg yolks, heavy cream, butter and sorghum in a nonreactive mixing bowl until smooth and well combined.

Fill the prepared tart shell with the custard, leaving about 1/4 inch of headspace to allow room for the filling to expand. For easy cleanup, place a sheet pan lined with foil on the rack below the tart to catch any custard overflow. Bake for 25 minutes. To check that the filling has set, gently shake the pan. If not set, continue to bake, rechecking every 5 minutes until just set. Cool on a wire rack. The tart may be made a day in advance and stored tightly wrapped in the refrigerator.

*(recipe continues)*

# CHOCOLATE SHORT DOUGH

MAKES FOUR 8- TO 9-INCH TART SHELLS

| | |
|---|---|
| I pound unsalted butter | 3¹/2 cups pastry flour |
| I¹/4 cups granulated sugar | ³/4 cup cocoa powder |
| 4 large eggs | |

In a large bowl, cream the butter with the sugar using a mixer or a wooden spoon. Add the eggs to the creamed butter, one at a time, until thoroughly incorporated. In anotehr bowl, sift together the flour and the cocoa powder. On a floured countertop, use your hands to combine the flour mixture with the creamed butter to form a rough dough. Use a gentle touch and try not to overwork the dough. Gather the dough into a ball, then flatten it into a disk. Wrap tightly in plastic wrap, and refrigerate until well chilled.

Preheat the oven to 350°F.

Divide the dough into four balls. Wrap three balls of dough individually in plastic and freeze for later use. Place the remaining ball of dough on a floured surface. Using a wooden rolling pin dusted with flour, roll into a round about 2 inches wider than your tart pan. Butter the inside of the pan and dust with flour. Roll the dough onto the rolling pin and transfer it by unrolling over the top of the pan. Gently press the dough into the tart pan, making sure that the sides and the bottom are fitted securely. Trim any excess dough with a sharp knife. Place a sheet of aluminum foil inside the tart dough, and weight with a handful of dried beans to prevent the shell from buckling while baking.

Bake for 10 minutes. Remove beans and foil and bake for 10 minutes longer, until the shell is lightly browned. Cool to room temperature before filling.

# PUMPKIN KUCHEN

Kuchen, a German word for cake, is used to denote a variety of Midwestern pastries. This recipe is similar to many that were handed down by families of German heritage in Minnesota, Wisconsin, Indiana, North Dakota, South Dakota and even as far west as Montana. In 2000, kuchen was named the official state dessert of South Dakota. Heartland's variation uses pumpkin instead of fruit as the featured ingredient.

3/4 pound (3 sticks) unsalted butter, softened

13/4 cups dark brown sugar

6 eggs

2 cups pumpkin purée

2 cups all-purpose flour

1 teaspoon cinnamon

1/2 teaspoon ground allspice

1/2 teaspoon ground ginger

2 teaspoons baking powder

1/2 teaspoon baking soda

1/2 teaspoon sea salt

Preheat the oven to 350°F. Cream together the butter and sugar with a mixer or wooden spoon. Incorporate the eggs one at a time, then stir in the pumpkin purée.

In separate bowl, sift together the flour, cinnamon, allspice, ginger, baking powder, baking soda and salt. Slowly add the dry ingredients to the butter mixture, mixing on low speed.

Butter and flour a 9-inch springform pan. Pour the batter into the pan. Gently tap the pan to eliminate air bubbles and level the batter. Bake for 35 to 40 minutes, until set and a toothpick inserted comes out clean. Allow the kuchen to cool completely on a rack at room temperature before releasing it from the pan.

# SUMMER CORN POTS DE CRÈME

Pot de crème is a very simple French dessert typically flavored with vanilla or chocolate. Heartland's version showcases a Minnesota summertime favorite, sweet corn. The variation with seasonal raspberries is just as delicious.

| | |
|---|---|
| 3 cups half and half | 2 large eggs |
| 3 cups raw corn kernels, puréed | 3 egg yolks |
| ¼ cup sugar | |

Preheat the oven to 325°F. Combine the half and half and corn purée in a nonreactive saucepan and bring to a boil over moderately high heat. Reduce heat to low and simmer for 5 minutes, until thickened. Remove from the heat.

In a large bowl, whisk the sugar with the eggs and egg yolks until well blended. Temper the sugar-egg mixture by gently stirring in ¼ cup warm corn puree. Continue to slowly add the remaining purée, taking care not to aerate the mixture. Divide among 6-ounce ovenproof ramekins.

Place the ramekins in a roasting pan, making sure that the tops of the ramekins are below the rim of the pan. Add hot water to the pan halfway up the sides of the ramekins. Cover the pan tightly with foil and punch some small holes in the top for steam to escape during baking.

Bake for 15 to 20 minutes, until set. Carefully remove ramekins from water, cool and refrigerate. Covered, the pots may be kept in the refrigerator for up to 3 days.

## VARIATION ON A THEME

To make **Raspberry Pots de Crème,** follow the recipe above, substituting 3 cups of fresh raspberries, pureed and strained, for the sweet corn puree.

# HOPE CREAMERY

Steele County, Minnesota, was once known as the Butter Capital of the World, because more butter was produced per square mile there than in any other place on earth. By the time Victor and Kelly Mrotz (right) bought Hope Creamery, things had changed quite a bit. The original 1920's red brick building was the last vestige of Steele County's butter heyday, when some thirty creameries were in full production, and it was in need of loving care.

Victor was raised in the shadow of that building and grew up eating Hope Creamery butter, but had long since relocated to the Twin Cities. After meeting his wife Kelly at a rock concert in Minneapolis, they started a family. In 2001, they moved to Hope, where they saved the old creamery by purchasing it.

That year, Victor brought me samples of Hope's freshly churned salted butter. It was good, but I needed an unsalted product—I couldn't cook with it if I couldn't regulate the salt content, and I also needed it for pastry production. In fact, I told Victor, I needed a locally produced high fat butter, with 85 percent butterfat content as opposed to the 82 percent that he was producing. He didn't let me down. Soon thereafter, I had an exclusive arrangement with Hope Creamery.

When Mega and I opened Heartland in its original location in October 2002, Hope Creamery and our special relationship came with us. We decided to use only the high fat for everything we did, including the butter served with freshly baked bread during dinner service.

We relocated in July 2009 and opened Heartland's attached Farm Direct Market. Of course, we wanted to sell Hope Creamery butter. The problem was that Victor and Kelly didn't have a retail label for the high fat butter since it was being produced exclusively for Heartland. Instead we filled the shelves with retail packages of their standard salted and unsalted butter. Then we created a special label for their one-pound prints of high fat butter so we could sell it out of our retail dairy case. A not-so-curious thing happened: No one wanted the standard butter. Everyone wanted the high fat, and today we have a hard time keeping it on the shelves.

# RASPBERRY PECAN LINZER TORTE

SERVES 8

Longtime Heartland pastry chef Jack Fulton and I share a keen appreciation for Austrian linzer torte, or linzertorte. It's traditionally served at Christmas in places with large populations of expat Germans, Austrians, Hungarians, Swiss and other central Europeans and their descendants. Minnesota is home to many ethnic Germans, and we take our linzer torte seriously.

The classic recipe calls for a flaky crust made with flour and ground nuts. To make our dough, we've sometimes used hazelnuts, which are common here, but we prefer Midwestern pecans grown in Kansas, Missouri and southern Illinois, which tend to be smaller and sweeter than Georgia's. We also add warm spices and cocoa powder to the dough, which smells festive. The classic linzer torte filling is always fruit jam or preserve, often a stone fruit or berry. Heartland's version uses raspberry jam topped simply with beautiful fresh raspberries, in place of the more traditional lattice of pastry strips.

I pound unsalted butter, preferably high fat, at room temperature

I cup plus I tablespoon (9¼ ounces) sugar

2 eggs

4 teaspoons cocoa powder

I tablespoon cinnamon

I teaspoon ground ginger

½ teaspoon ground nutmeg

3½ cups (I pound) all-purpose flour

¾ teaspoon baking powder

1¼ cups (10½ ounces) pecans, finely chopped

3 cups Raspberry Jam

4 cups raspberries

Butter and flour for dusting

Preheat the oven to 375°F. To make the shell, in the bowl of stand mixer fitted with the paddle attachment, cream the butter with the sugar on moderately low speed. While continuing to mix, add the eggs one at a time until incorporated.

In a large mixing bowl, sift together the cocoa, cinnamon, ginger, nutmeg, flour and baking powder, and slowly add to the butter mixture. Change out the mixer's paddle and replace it with a dough hook. Slowly incorporate the pecans until thoroughly combined.

On a lightly floured work surface, roll out the linzer dough into a 12-inch round. Fit the dough into the bottom of a 10-inch springform pan that has been lightly buttered and dusted with flour. Trim off the excess dough and set it aside.

Use the reserved dough to roll pea-sized balls, and use them to line the outside wall of the pan, forming a circle. Repeat this process with the remaining balls of dough, forming a smaller concentric circle toward the center of the pan. Chill in the refrigerator for about 10 minutes.

When fully chilled, place the pan in the oven and prebake the crust for 12 minutes. Allow it to cool on a wire rack.

Fill the open space between the two rows of dough balls with most of the raspberry jam, reserving 2 tablespoons. If the jam has gelled, warm it briefly over low heat until it liquefies enough to become pourable. Return the pan to the oven, and bake the torte for 15 minutes, until the jam just begins to bubble. Remove the pan from the oven, and return it to a wire rack to cool.

Complete the torte by arranging fresh raspberries in concentric circles on top of the jam. Using a pastry brush, glaze the raspberries with the reserved jam. If the jam is too thick to adhere to the brush, add a little water while stirring it over low heat.

Refrigerate the torte for about 10 minutes before serving. To serve, release the latch on the springform pan and carefully transfer the torte to a serving dish using a metal spatula. Cut into eight slices, and serve with sweetened whipped cream.

## RASPBERRY JAM

MAKES 3 CUPS

Here's a quick and easy raspberry jam that uses no fruit pectin to help the jam set. This is significant since the linzer torte filling needs to spend a few minutes in the oven, and pectin acts funny when it is reheated. This recipe uses only two ingredients, but it requires the cook to pay close attention.

| 4 cups granulated sugar | 4 cups raspberries |
|---|---|

Preheat the oven to 250° F. Place the sugar in an ovenproof bowl and warm it in the oven for 15 minutes. This will help it dissolve more easily.

Bring the raspberries to a boil in a large nonreactive saucepan over moderately high heat, mashing them occasionally. Make sure the saucepan will hold at least twice

the volume of berries since they will double in size when heated. Once the berries have reached a boil, boil for 1 minute while stirring constantly. Stir in the sugar and continue to boil until the jam begins to gel, about 5 minutes. Continue stirring during this time so the jam doesn't scorch or stick to the bottom of the pan.

To determine when the mixture has formed a gel, use the simple spoon test: Working quickly, dip a teaspoon into the pan, remove and turn it sideways so that the jam drips off the spoon. Keep doing this every minute or two until the drops are very thick and begin to run together before falling off the spoon. When that happens, the jam is ready, so remove the pan from the heat. The jam may now be poured into the torte, or set aside for later use. It keeps well in the refrigerator for up to one month.

# WILD RICE MADELEINES

Proust's iconic cookie gets a Midwestern accent with earthy local wild rice flour. These taste best when freshly baked and still warm, with a dusting of powdered sugar clinging to their golden edges. However, they can be kept at room temperature for up to one week in an airtight container.

To create cake flour, subtract 2 tablespoons from 1 level cup of all-purpose flour and replace with 2 tablespoons cornstarch. Whisk to combine before using.

6 large eggs

I cup minus I tablespoon (7 ounces) sugar

½ cup (4 ounces) wild rice flour

6 tablespoons (3 ounces) cake flour

I teaspoon baking powder

¾ cup unsalted butter

Butter and flour for dusting

In a large bowl or stand mixer, whip the eggs with the sugar to full volume until thick. In another bowl, sift together the wild rice flour, cake flour and baking powder. Fold the egg and sugar mixture into the dry ingredients until well incorporated. Melt the butter, and fold into the batter. Refrigerate for about 20 minutes.

Preheat the oven to 400° F. Grease a madeleine pan and dust it with flour. Scoop 1 rounded tablespoon of batter into each madeleine mold.

Bake for 8 minutes or until the madeleines set. Remove the pan from the oven, and turn out onto a rack while still warm.

# CRANBERRY SHORTCAKE

SERVES 8

This is a simple, delicious shortcake that is best enjoyed with morning coffee or afternoon tea. It can also be dressed up with fresh berries and sweetened whipped cream for a light yet satisfying dessert.

We sometimes substitute vanilla sugar for the granulated sugar. It is easily prepared by slicing a vanilla bean lengthwise and burying it in a couple of cups of sugar in an airtight container at room temperature. Let it sit for about a week. Note the cranberries macerate for 8 hours.

1¹/2 cups (12 ounces) cake flour

1¹/2 cups (12 ounces) bread flour

3/4 cup (6 ounces) sugar

2 tablespoons plus 1 teaspoon baking powder

1 teaspoon salt

1 pound cold unsalted whole butter, cut into small cubes

1 pound dried cranberries, soaked overnight in red wine to cover

3/4 cup heavy cream

Butter and flour for dusting

In a large bowl, sift together the cake flour, bread flour, sugar, baking powder and salt. Add the butter and use your fingertips to work it into the dry ingredients to form coarse, grain-like balls.

Drain the cranberries, reserving 1 tablespoon of the wine. Add the cranberries to the dough. Using your hands or a mixer with the paddle attachment on low speed, slowly add the cream and the reserved wine. Combine to make a stiff dough.

Preheat the oven to 375° F. On a lightly floured work surface, pat the dough into two rectangular loaves 8 inches long. Cut each loaf into 4 equal pieces. Place the shortcakes on 2 lightly greased baking sheets dusted with flour. Bake the shortcakes for 30 to 40 minutes, or until a toothpick inserted in the center comes out clean. Remove them from the oven, transfer the shortcakes to a rack and allow to cool.

# CHOCOLATE MAPLE ROULADE

At Heartland, we use maple syrup in much the same way as we do sorghum syrup. This lovely dessert pairs chocolate with maple syrup to create a mousse that we roll inside chocolate sponge cake to form a roulade. As is standard in pastry kitchens, we weigh the dry ingredients rather than measure them.

**FOR THE SPONGE**

12 eggs, separated

7/8 cup (7 ounces) maple syrup

1/2 cup (4 ounces) cake flour

1/2 cup minus 1 tablespoon (3 1/2 ounces) cocoa powder

7/8 cup (7 ounces) sugar, plus more for dusting

**FOR THE MOUSSE**

10 ounces dark chocolate, chopped

5 egg yolks

3/4 cup maple syrup

2 cups cold heavy cream

Preheat the oven to 350°F. To make the chocolate sponge cake, whip the egg yolks in a stand mixer until doubled in volume. While the yolks are whipping, bring the maple syrup to the boil in a saucepan over moderately high heat. Simmer until reduced by half. Pour the hot maple syrup into the whipping egg yolks. Whip until cool and set aside.

In a bowl, sift together the flour and cocoa. In a clean mixer bowl, combine the egg whites and sugar and whisk to form soft peaks. Fold one third of the yolk mixture into the egg whites. Fold the flour and cocoa into the egg mixture, and then fold in the remaining egg whites. Line a sheet pan with parchment, and spread the batter evenly over the pan. Bake until set, about 20 minutes.

To make the mousse, melt the chocolate in a bowl set over a pan of simmering water. Place the egg yolks in the bowl of a stand mixer and whisk until doubled in volume.

Bring the maple syrup to the boil in a saucepan over moderately high heat. Simmer until reduced by half. With the mixer running, pour the hot maple syrup in a steady stream into the egg yolks. Transfer to a mixing bowl and fold in the melted chocolate.

In a large bowl, whip the cream to medium peaks, and fold it gently into the chocolate mixture. Transfer the mousse to a bowl and refrigerate until set.

When the cake has cooled to room temperature, dust the top with sugar and turn it out onto a sheet of parchment. Spread the mousse evenly over the cake. Using parchment, roll the cake tightly. Refrigerate until firm. Slice with a long serrated knife.

# UNCLE GILLY'S MAPLE SYRUP

The limestone-rich section of southwestern Wisconsin known as the Driftless Area extends into Minnesota, Iowa and extreme northwestern Illinois, and is characterized by a geography that escaped glaciation. Magnificent river bluffs and eroded plateaus are bisected by rivers and streams that sometimes disappear underground into a warren of cave systems. It's where the Upper Midwest's burgeoning wine industry is located, and is also a superb habitat for our native trout.

Gil and Justine Vernon raise maple trees on 80 acres of hills in Dunn County, in the Driftless, and produce small batch maple syrup so dark it is nearly opaque. Once the trees begin their early spring thaw with warm daytime temperatures followed by subfreezing nights, the sap begins to flow. Maple trees have a unique cell structure that allows the sap to move horizontally as well as vertically, so they are ideal for natural gravity tapping.

The Vernons gather this sap in buckets and transport it to their sugar shack. Contrary to its humble name, the shack is a beautiful structure of red pine timbers and panels harvested from their land, then milled on a sawmill Gil built from a kit. There, the whole family (including sons Nate and Justin, of the Grammy-winning band Bon Iver, and daughter Kim and her family) congregates for late-night marathons of sap boiling and tending the wood fire. The longer it spends on the fire, the darker the syrup gets, and it takes 40 gallons of sap to produce one gallon of syrup. Calculated by drips from the tree, there are 750,000 drips in every quart of Uncle Gilly's Maple Syrup.

# CHESTNUT PANNA COTTA
## WITH HONEY OAT TUILES

SERVES 8

Instead of using eggs to bind the custard, as in a pot de crème, panna cotta calls for a small amount of gelatin. Like pots de crème, it is often flavored with vanilla or chocolate. Our Minnesota version uses sweetened chestnut purée with a touch of vanilla.

Chestnuts remind of my high school days, when I would skip school to cross the river from my home in, New Jersey to Manhattan. I'd visit a museum or the United Nations, head uptown to Harlem or downtown to the Bottom Line to hear live jazz. In the mid-70s, punk and new wave music was just beginning, and I saw some bands that became legends. On cold winter days, I'd do what my mother had taught me to do: find the nearest street vendor selling roasted chestnuts, and fill my pockets to keep my hands warm. Once they cooled off, I had a tasty snack.

I ³/4 cups heavy cream

¹/2 cup whole milk

4 ounces sweetened chestnut purée

¹/2 vanilla bean, split lengthwise

2 5-gram gelatin leaves or one .25-ounce envelope gelatin powder

Honey Oat Tuiles

In a medium nonreactive saucepan, whisk the cream, milk and chestnut purée. Scrape the seeds from the vanilla bean and add with the pod to the mixture. Bring just to the boil, then remove from the heat.

Meanwhile, soak the gelatin leaves in water until soft, 2 to 3 minutes. Drain the leaves, making sure to squeeze out any excess water. Add the gelatin to the saucepan and allow to dissolve. Strain the mixture through a fine-mesh sieve and cool to room temperature. Divide evenly among 8 4- or 5-inch ramekins and refrigerate for at least 4 hours. Unmold and garnish with Honey Oat Tuiles.

*(recipe continues)*

# HONEY OAT TUILES

MAKES ABOUT 4 DOZEN COOKIES

This is a simple recipe for a crisp cookie tuile flavored with honey and rolled oats. It's nice to serve these with a pot de crème or panna cotta, or enjoy them with a cup of tea or coffee. Pastry flour is more finely milled than all-purpose flour, and results in a crisper tuile.

| | |
|---|---|
| 1 cup unsalted butter, softened to room temperature | 3/4 cup honey |
| 1 cup sugar | 1/4 cup light corn syrup |
| 3/4 cup cake flour | Scant 3/4 cup rolled oats |

Preheat the oven to 425°F. In a stand mixer fitted with the paddle attachment or in a mixing bowl with a wooden spoon, cream together the butter and sugar. Add the flour, honey, corn syrup and oats. Mix until well combined.

Generously butter a large baking sheet. Drop rounded teaspoons of the batter 4 inches apart on prepared pan. With the back of a spoon, spread batter into 2-inch rounds. Bake for 4 to 6 minutes, or until the edges turn golden brown. Using a spatula, immediately transfer the tuiles to a rolling pin, and allow them to cool in curved shapes. The tuiles may be made a day ahead and kept in an airtight container.

---

## AMERICAN CHESTNUT PLIGHT

True chestnut trees are native to Europe, Asia and North America. Around 1900, a fungus blight, to which the Asian or Chinese chestnut is generally immune, was unknowingly imported to the United States. Almost all native American chestnut trees were wiped out; only a few trees, blight-resistant by virtue of a genetic anomaly, survived. Given that chestnuts were a primary source of protein for black bears, large populations of bears suffered and died from malnutrition.

Over the years, the American Chestnut Foundation has worked to restore the chestnut tree to North America by crossing descendants of our native trees with hardy Chinese varieties. While these efforts are primarily focused on reestablishing the lumber industry, work is being done at Badgersett Research Farm in Canton, Minnesota, for the sole purpose of producing high-quality edible nuts. At Heartland we use large quantities of nuts from that farm, but chances are the chestnuts you buy in your local grocery or market were imported from Italy.

# HONEY POACHED PLUMS
## WITH CANDIED PECANS

As a boy, I was never drawn to elaborate sweets or the finely crafted Italian pastries from Carlo's in Hoboken that often graced our family's table. Instead, I gravitated toward fruit, and I still do.

2 cups dry red wine

1/2 cup honey

Bouquet garni (1 cinnamon stick, 1 bay leaf, 5 whole allspice, 10 black peppercorns)

1 pound black plums, halved and pitted

Candied Pecans

Combine the wine and honey in a nonreactive saucepan. Add the bouquet garni and bring to a boil. Reduce the heat and add the plums. Cook gently until the plums soften, about 3 minutes. Strain the plums through a fine-mesh sieve, reserving the poaching liquid. Return the liquid to the pot and reduce until slightly syrupy. Pour the syrup over the plums. Serve with Candied Pecans.

## CANDIED PECANS

### MAKES ABOUT 4 CUPS

The salty-sweet crunch of these nuts goes well with any delicate poached fruit. This recipe calls for pecans, which Heartland sources from Missouri and a small corner of southern Illinois, but we have used blanched and peeled hazelnuts, as well as walnuts.

1 egg white

1 tablespoon water

1 pound pecan halves

1 cup sugar

1 teaspoon sea salt

1/2 teaspoon ground cinnamon

Preheat the oven to 250° F. In a stainless steel mixing bowl, whip the egg white and water until frothy. Add the pecans and stir to coat them evenly.

In a separate bowl, combine the sugar, salt and cinnamon. Remove the nuts from the egg white and toss in the sugar mixture until well coated. Spread the nuts out on a greased sheet pan. Bake for 1 hour, stirring every 15 minutes to ensure even cooking. Remove from the oven and allow the nuts to cool. Store in an airtight container.

# PUMPKIN SEED FRANGIPANE TART
## WITH BRANDIED PRUNES

Pumpkin seeds are ubiquitous in our kitchen. We use them in everything from mole'
sauce to pestos and vinaigrettes. Toasted pumpkin seeds add crunch to salads, and are
sometimes ground into a powder to mix with flour as a crust for fried fish. Here they
replace the more expected almonds in a frangipane filling for a really fine autumn tart.

1/2 pound pumpkin seeds

7/8 cup sugar

2 tablespoons light corn syrup

1 tablespoon water

1 prebaked 9-inch Tart Shell

1 pound Brandied Prunes

1/4 cup Brandied Prunes poaching
liquid, reduced to a syrup

Preheat the oven to 350°F. To make the frangipane filling, purée the pumpkin seeds,
sugar, corn syrup and water in a food processor to form a paste.

Spread the frangipane evenly over the bottom of a prebaked 9-inch tart shell.
It should be about 1/2 inch thick. Arrange the prunes in a single layer on top of the
frangipane. Bake for 45 minutes or until the frangipane is set and lightly browned. It
should be soft to the touch with a crusty exterior. Remove the tart from the oven, and set
on a cooling rack.

In a small saucepan, reduce the prune poaching liquid by half. Baste the cooled tart
with the prune syrup. Wait at least 10 minutes before removing the outer ring of the tart
mold. Use a flexible knife to free the tart by slipping it between the tart and the bottom of
the mold, then slide the tart onto the cooling rack. Allow to cool completely before slicing
with a serrated knife.

## TART SHELL

This recipe makes two shells. Use one for this recipe and store the dough for the second
in the freezer, well wrapped, for up to one month. To easily transfer dough from the work
surface, first roll it up loosely on your rolling pin, then unfurl it onto the tart pan.

1¼ pounds (5 sticks) unsalted butter, at room temperature

1 cup powdered sugar

2 egg yolks

2 tablespoons milk

½ teaspoon sea salt

1 teaspoon vanilla extract

5 cups all-purpose flour

In the bowl of a stand mixer, combine the butter and sugar, and cream together on low speed. Add the egg yolks and blend well. Beat in the milk, salt and vanilla. Mix in the flour just until incorporated. Transfer the dough to a floured cutting board, and cover with a towel or plastic wrap. Refrigerate until firm, about 1 hour.

Preheat the oven to 350°F. Generously grease and flour a 9-inch tart pan. Roll out the tart dough to about 12 inches in diameter. Press the dough firmly into the mold and cut off the overlapping dough with a sharp knife. Gently pierce the bottom of the tart dough with the tines of a fork. Cover with a circular piece of parchment and top with a thin layer of beans or pie weights to prevent the shell from buckling during baking. Prebake for 10 minutes or until it just begins to turn brown. Remove the tart crust from the oven, and allow it cool to room temperature. Once the tart crust is cool, remove the beans and parchment and proceed with the recipe.

## BRANDIED PRUNES

MAKES 2 POUNDS

1 cup water

½ cup brandy

½ cup plus 1 tablespoon sugar

1 cinnamon stick

1 vanilla bean, split lengthwise

5 whole cloves

2½ pounds prunes, pitted

Combine the water, brandy, sugar, cinnamon, vanilla and cloves in a large pot and bring to a boil over moderately high heat. Add the prunes. Remove from the stove and let the prunes cool to room temperature. Refrigerate in the poaching liquid until ready to use.

# HONEY GOAT CHEESE GATEAUX
## WITH RED CURRANT COULIS

〉 SERVES 6 〈

We make these delicate individual fresh goat cheese cakes for dessert when fresh currants are available, and also when we raid the freezer for those currants we put away during their all-too-brief season. Any light-bodied honey may be substituted for the wildflower.

22 ounces fresh chèvre, at room temperature

1/2 cup wildflower honey plus 6 teaspoons

6 tablespoons sugar

2 egg yolks

1 large egg

Red Currant Coulis

Using a stand or hand mixer, cream the goat cheese with 1/2 cup honey and the sugar. With the mixer running, add the egg yolks and the whole egg one at time until well blended. Make sure to scrape the side of the bowl with a rubber spatula.

Preheat the oven to 350° F. Place six 4-ounce ramekins in a baking dish. Place 1 teaspoon of honey in each ramekin. Divide the batter among the ramekins. Fill the baking dish with enough cold water to reach halfway up the side of the ramekins. Make sure the ramekins are not touching each other or the sides of the dish. Bake for 15 to 18 minutes or until the gâteaux are set. Let cool and refrigerate for 8 hours.

Unmold the gâteaux by running a sharp knife around the edge of each ramekin and carefully flip onto individual serving plates. Serve with red currant coulis.

## RED CURRANT COULIS

MAKES ABOUT 2 CUPS

4 cups fresh red currants, stemmed

3/4 cup sugar

3/4 cup water

Using a blender or food processor, purée the currants. Pass the puree through a fine mesh sieve to remove the seeds and skins, using a wooden spoon to scrape the puree through.

In a heavy nonreactive saucepan, combine sugar with the water and bring to a boil over moderately high heat. Stir until the sugar dissolves. Allow the syrup to cool to room temperature. Add 3/4 cup of the syrup to the strained currant purée and stir to combine. The coulis will keep for up to 2 months in the refrigerator.

# CORNMEAL MARSALA–RAISIN BISCOTTI

If you ever find yourself in Prato, Italy, the birthplace of biscotti, you might see these little biscuits referred to as cantucci or coffee bread. Whatever you call them, biscotti with a cup of espresso is a nice way to start the day. We incorporate cornmeal into the batter to give these traditional Tuscan biscotti a little bit of Minnesota texture.

I cup sugar

1¼ cups all-purpose flour

1¼ cups coarsely ground cornmeal

½ teaspoon baking powder

½ teaspoon sea salt

6 ounces dark raisins or Zante currants soaked in marsala

2 egg yolks

2 eggs

Preheat the oven to 350°F. Combine the sugar, flour, cornmeal, baking powder and salt on a large wooden board. Drain the raisins, reserving the marsala, and add to the dry mixture. Form a well in the center of the mixture, and add the eggs and egg yolks with about 1 tablespoon of the reserved marsala. Using a fork, incorporate the wet and dry ingredients, and lightly knead until the dough comes together.

Divide the dough into thirds and form into rectangular loaves. Place the loaves on a baking pan lined with parchment, and bake for 30 minutes or until firm to the touch. Remove from the oven and cool to room temperature.

Slice the loaves crosswise ½ inch thick and lay cut side up on the baking sheet. Return to the oven and bake for 5 to 10 minutes or until dry. Transfer to a rack to cool. Store the biscotti in an airtight container.

# CLASSIC BUTTERMILK FLAPJACKS

This recipe and its apple sidekick pay tribute to Paul Bunyan, whose unrelenting hunger for flapjacks is part of his Minnesota legend. It's always a good time to make a batch, so bring on the maple syrup.

| | |
|---|---|
| 2¹/2 cups all-purpose flour | ¹/2 cup honey |
| 1¹/2 cups whole wheat flour | 4 eggs |
| 2 tablespoons baking powder | 2 tablespoons grapeseed oil |
| 2 cups buttermilk | Melted butter, for cooking the pancakes |

Sift together the all-purpose and whole-wheat flours into a large bowl and combine with the baking powder.

In another bowl, combine the buttermilk, honey, eggs and oil until well blended. Slowly add the flour mixture to the wet ingredients until well incorporated. It is not necessary for the batter to be completely smooth.

To cook the pancakes, heat a griddle or large skillet over moderately high heat. Brush with the melted butter and use a small ladle to pour about 1/4 cup of batter for each pancake. Cook for about 3 minutes on each side, turning when small bubbles appear on the surface of the pancake.

## BUCKWHEAT APPLE FLAPJACKS

| | |
|---|---|
| 1 cup buckwheat flour | ¹/2 cup honey |
| 1¹/2 cups all-purpose flour | 4 eggs |
| 1¹/2 cups whole wheat flour | 2 tablespoons grapeseed oil |
| 2 tablespoons baking powder | 2 cups peeled and diced apples |
| 2 cups buttermilk | Melted unsalted butter, for cooking the pancakes |

Sift together the buckwheat, all-purpose and whole wheat flours into a large bowl and combine with the baking powder.

In another bowl, combine the buttermilk, honey, eggs and oil until well blended. Slowly add the flour mixture to the wet ingredients until well incorporated. Stir in the apples. It is not necessary for the batter to be completely smooth.

To cook, heat a griddle or large skillet over moderately high heat. Brush with the melted butter and use a small ladle to pour about ¼ cup of batter. Cook for about 3 minutes on each side, turning when small bubbles appear on the surface of the pancake.

## PAUL BUNYAN AND SOURDOUGH SAM

American folklore holds that the mythical lumberjack Paul Bunyan was born in Bangor, Maine, but don't tell that to anyone around here.

Minnesota boasts at least four sizable Bunyan monuments. A 26-foot-tall talking statue greets visitors in Brainerd, home of the Paul Bunyan Land theme park. In Akeley, you can sit in the palm of a 25-foot Bunyan's extended hand. Bemidji is home to another giant statue, plus his ax, his pet dog, his pet squirrel, his razor, his toothpaste, his telephone and his Zippo lighter. Yes, Paul Bunyan had a phone and a Zippo lighter. His anchor is in Ortonville, and his rifle is in Black Duck. In Hackensack stands a 17-foot statue of his girlfriend, Lucette Diana Kensack, erected in 1991.

According to legend, Bunyan's sidekick, Babe the Blue Ox, turned that color after an especially cold winter. One tale claims Paul dug out the Great Lakes to give Babe a proper watering hole, and another that the Land of 10,000 Lakes was created from the footprints of Paul and Babe wandering aimlessly in a blizzard. Some insist the lakes are the result of Babe pushing down tree stumps left over after Paul had harvested the lumber of the North Woods.

Paul and his ax men ate so many flapjacks that the trail cook, Sourdough Sam, couldn't keep up with their demand. Big Ole, the camp blacksmith, made a griddle so big you couldn't see across it once it began to smoke. Sam had 50 men with pork rinds tied to their feet skating around the griddle to grease it, and he mixed the flapjack batter in large barrels. It took several strong cooks just to flip the flapjacks and several more to get them to the table.

Paul Bunyan is buried in Kelliher, Minnesota, where his grave is marked with the inscription, "Here lies Paul, and that is all."

# BUTTERMILK BISCUITS

This is my favorite biscuit recipe. I've used it for years. It makes perfect biscuits. Enjoy with some farmstead butter and your favorite honey. Or slice the biscuits in half and pile high with sliced strawberries or peaches, and plenty of freshly whipped cream.

1 cup plus 1½ teaspoons all-purpose flour

2½ teaspoons baking powder

½ teaspoon baking soda

½ teaspoon sea salt

1 tablespoon sugar

½ cup cold buttermilk

¼ cup cold heavy cream

1 large egg

2½ ounces cold lard or butter, cut into ½-inch cubes, plus extra for baking

Extra flour, for dusting

Preheat the oven to 400°F. Sift the flour, baking powder, baking soda, salt and sugar into a large bowl. In another bowl, combine the buttermilk and cream. Whisk the egg into the cream mixture until well incorporated.

Add the lard to the flour mixture and, using your fingertips, rub together to form pea-sized pieces. With your hands or a wooden spoon, quickly mix the dry and liquid ingredients together to form a soft dough.

Dust a work surface with a small handful of flour. Turn the dough and gently knead for 1 minute. Do not overmix or your biscuits will be tough.

Pat the dough flat. Using a rolling pin, roll out to a thickness of ¾ inch to 1 inch. Cut into 2-inch rounds using a cookie cutter or a small glass. Make sure to dust the cutter with flour so it doesn't stick to the dough.

Lightly grease a baking sheet with additional lard. Arrange the biscuits on the baking sheet about 2 inches apart. Bake for 18 to 22 minutes or until deep golden brown.

# SPICY OATMEAL CRACKERS

I enjoy telling visitors to Heartland that it's easier to think of what we don't make from scratch than what we do. We make many thousands of crackers every year, and serve them with soups and appetizers as well as our local cheese selection. Crackers are fairly simple and fun to make, they keep well and you can cut them into any shape or size.

¾ pound (3 sticks) unsalted butter, softened

½ cup sugar

1½ cups steel-cut oats

2 pounds plus 10 ounces bread flour

2 teaspoons sea salt

2 teaspoons baking soda

1 teaspoon cayenne pepper

2 teaspoons paprika

Preheat the oven to 325°F. In a large bowl, combine the butter and sugar. In another bowl, combine the oats, flour, salt, baking soda, cayenne and paprika. Add to the butter mixture. Mix until the dough just comes together. Do not over-mix or crackers will be too flat when baked.

Divide the dough into four equal portions, and roll each part on a floured cutting board to the length and width of one full sheet pan (18" x 26"). Score and cut the cracker dough to any desired size. Bake on parchment-lined sheet pans for 30 minutes or until light golden brown. Transfer to wire racks to cool. Store in an airtight container.

# WILD RICE CRACKERS

2 tablespoons active dry yeast

1 1/2 cups warm water

2 cups whole wheat flour

1 cup all-purpose flour

1/2 cup wild rice flour

1/2 cup finely ground cornmeal

1 teaspoon sea salt

2 teaspoons freshly ground
black pepper

In a large mixing bowl, dissolve the yeast in the warm water. Set aside for 5 minutes or until the yeast begins to bubble. Meanwhile, sift together the whole wheat, all-purpose and rice flours with the cornmeal. Stir in the salt and pepper. Add the flour mixture to the yeast. Mix well until the dough is pliable but not sticky.

Transfer the dough to an oiled bowl, and cover it with a clean kitchen towel. Set aside to rise at room temperature for 1 hour. Remove the towel, and punch down the dough. Let the dough rest for 20 minutes.

Preheat the oven to 400°F. Line a half-sheet pan (18″ × 26″) with parchment. Roll the dough on a lightly floured surface to the length and width of the pan. Score and cut the cracker dough to any desired size.

Transfer to the sheet pan. Bake for 30 minutes or until light golden brown. Transfer to a wire rack to cool. Store in an airtight container.

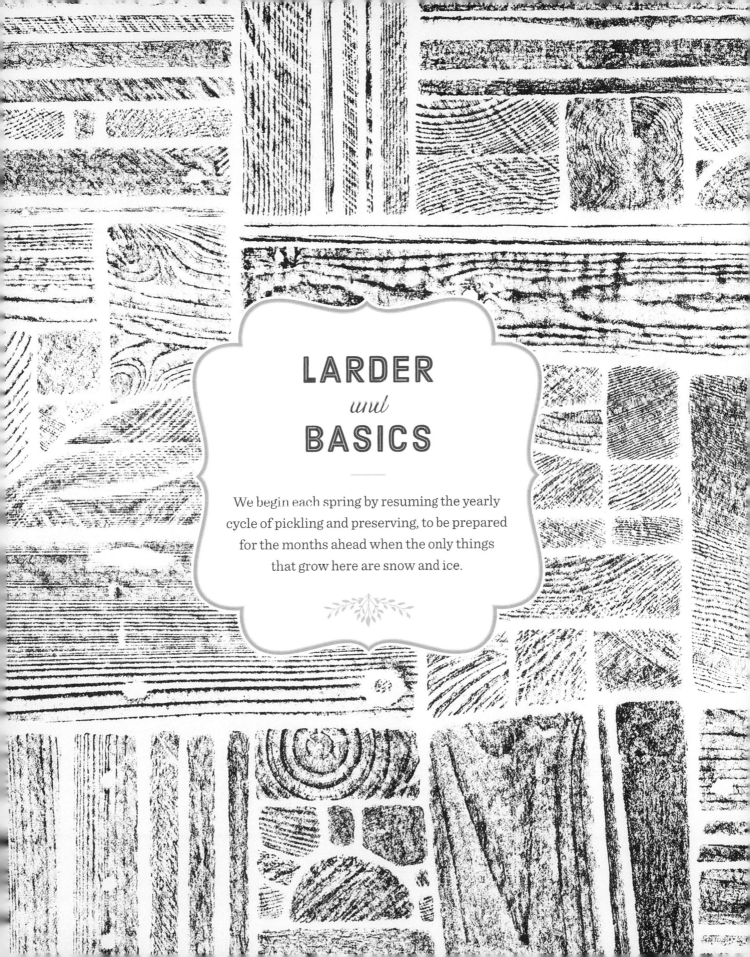

# LARDER
*und*
# BASICS

We begin each spring by resuming the yearly
cycle of pickling and preserving, to be prepared
for the months ahead when the only things
that grow here are snow and ice.

# LARDER
*and*
## BASICS

# HONEYCRISP APPLE MUSTARD

At Heartland, we create many different mustards, but the base is always the same. When selecting mustard seeds, which come in black and yellow varieties, feel free to use what's readily available—both produce an excellent condiment. For this recipe, I prefer black mustard seeds, which are Middle Eastern in origin. Their flavor profile is stronger and more pungent. Yellow mustard seeds, probably originating in the eastern Mediterranean, are best in vinaigrettes and relishes where their less assertive nature is matched to food of milder flavors.

| | |
|---|---|
| 12 Honeycrisp or other small apples (about 3 pounds) | 6 tablespoons chopped shallots |
| 2 cups water | 1 tablespoon freshly ground black pepper |
| 1 cup black mustard seeds | 1/2 teaspoon ground allspice |
| 1 cup mustard powder | 1 teaspoon ground cinnamon |
| 3 cups apple cider vinegar | 1/4 teaspoon ground cloves |
| 6 tablespoons wildflower honey | 1 teaspoon ground mace |
| 6 tablespoons sorghum syrup | 1 teaspoon sea salt |
| 2 tablespoons chopped garlic | |

Preheat the oven to 350°F. Core, peel and dice the apples. Place on a baking sheet and roast until soft, about 15 minutes.

Bring the water to a boil in a nonreactive saucepan. Add the mustard seeds and mustard powder. Reduce the heat to moderate and add the vinegar, honey, sorghum syrup, garlic, shallots, pepper, allspice, cinnamon, cloves, mace, salt and roasted apples. Simmer for 10 minutes, then remove from the heat and cool.

Carefully transfer the mustard to a blender in batches, if necessary, and purée until smooth. Scrape into clean glass jars, cover and refrigerate for up to 4 weeks.

## VARIATIONS ON A THEME

**For Apricot, Plum or Raspberry Mustard**, substitute 1 pint of pureed apricots, plums or raspberries for the apples. Use raspberry vinegar instead of the apple cider vinegar.

**For Chili Pepper Mustard**, substitute 1/4 cup pickled chili peppers for the apples.

**For Fennel Mustard**, substitute 1 cup chopped fennel fronds for the apples.

# STONE FRUIT CATSUP

MAKES ABOUT 4 PINTS

Catsup, or ketchup, is thought to have evolved from a fish-based Asian dipping sauce, which was altered in the early days of the newly independent American colonies to feature a native fruit. That fruit, of course, is the tomato. I call my version "catsup" in order to embrace all of the possibilities that seasonal stone fruits—plums, peaches and apricots—bring to this humble condiment. Try it as a condiment with cheese.

Stone fruits have a higher sugar content and lower acidity than tomatoes, so we sometimes add both sweet and dry wines, either white or red, or in combination.

5 quarts ripe plums, peaches or apricots, halved, stoned and roughly chopped

1¼ cups light brown sugar, packed

2 cups apple cider vinegar

2 cups wine

6 garlic cloves

I cup chopped sweet onion

1½ cinnamon sticks

2 teaspoons grated fresh ginger

2½ teaspoons ground allspice

2½ teaspoons ground mace

2½ teaspoons ground nutmeg

½ teaspoon ground cloves

¾ cup sea salt

2 teaspoons cayenne pepper

2½ teaspoons freshly ground black pepper

I bay leaf

Place the fruit in a large nonreactive pot with the sugar, vinegar and wine. Bring to a simmer over moderately-low heat. Add the garlic and onions and simmer for 5 more minutes. Stir in the cinnamon, ginger, allspice, mace, nutmeg, cloves, salt, cayenne pepper, black pepper and bay leaves. Continue to simmer until the catsup thickens to the consistency of heavy cream, about 20 to 25 minutes.

Remove the bay leaves and cinnamon sticks. Transfer the catsup in batches if necessary to a blender or food processor and purée until smooth. Refrigerate until cool. The natural pectin in the fruit will continue to thicken the sauce. Transfer to clean jars or containers, cover tightly and refrigerate for up to 4 weeks.

## VARIATION ON A THEME

For **Raspberry Catsup**, substitute raspberries and raspberry vinegar for the stone fruit and apple cider vinegar along with a dry red wine.

# TOMATO CATSUP

We use heirloom varieties of paste and plum tomatoes, and sometimes even green tomatoes, to make the classic tomato-based catsup. Because tomatoes are already high in acid, we omit the wine.

Much depends on the water content of the tomatoes you start with, so appraise them thoughtfully. Tomato plants act like a pump, driving water to the fruit. That is why you will sometimes see the skins of tomatoes crack if they are subject to overwatering or too much rain. Water content varies depending on the time of year a tomato is harvested and the weather during that particular growing season, as well as the variety. Because paste, plum and Roma tomatoes have significantly more pulp than slicing tomatoes, they are my first choice for this recipe. Otherwise, add a little tomato paste to help achieve the consistency you desire. Simply cooking the catsup down until it is thick enough is a risky proposition. The sugars will eventually begin to burn, and that will spoil the batch.

5 quarts very ripe paste, plum or Roma tomatoes, halved lengthwise

1¼ cups light brown sugar, packed

4 cups apple cider vinegar

6 garlic cloves

I cup chopped onion

1½ cinnamon sticks

2 teaspoons grated fresh ginger, grated

2½ teaspoons ground allspice

2½ teaspoons ground mace

2½ teaspoons ground nutmeg

½ teaspoon ground cloves

¾ cup sea salt

2 teaspoons cayenne pepper

2½ teaspoons freshly ground black pepper

I bay leaf

Combine the tomatoes in a large nonreactive pot with the sugar and vinegar. Bring to a simmer over moderately low heat. Add the garlic and onions and simmer for 5 minutes. Stir in the cinnamon, ginger, allspice, mace, nutmeg, cloves, salt, cayenne pepper, black pepper and bay leaf. Continue to simmer until the catsup thickens to the consistency of heavy cream, about 20 to 25 minutes.

Remove the bay leaf and cinnamon sticks. Transfer the catsup, in batches if necessary, to a blender or food processor and purée until smooth. Refrigerate until cool. The natural pectin in the fruit will continue to thicken the sauce.

Transfer to clean jars, cover tightly and refrigerate for up to 4 weeks.

# FRESH CRANBERRY SAUCE

This recipes pay tribute to our neighbor, Wisconsin, the number one cranberry-producing state in the country. Heartland uses both fresh and preserved cranberries as well as cranberry juice in many of our recipes. Next Thanksgiving, instead of buying cranberry sauce in a can, try this. If you can't wait that long, serve with grilled or roast pork. I promise you won't be disappointed.

| | |
|---|---|
| 1 pound fresh cranberries | 1 cup sugar |
| 2 cups fresh orange cubes, skin on | 1/2 cup water |
| 1 tablespoon grated fresh ginger | 1/4 cup Grand Marnier |
| 1 cinnamon stick | |

Place half of the cranberries and the oranges, ginger, cinnamon, sugar, water and Grand Marnier in a nonreactive saucepan. Bring to a simmer over moderate heat and cook until the cranberries soften and begin to pop. Add the remaining cranberries, and cook for 3 minutes longer.

Remove from the heat, transfer to a nonreactive container and discard the cinnamon stick. Place the container in the refrigerator, and allow the sauce to cool. The sauce will thicken once it is cold, and it may be served immediately or refrigerated for up to two weeks in a covered container.

# CARAWAY SAUERKRAUT

Cabbages of all kinds are a staple of the Heartland kitchen. For us, cabbage means sauerkraut—a cornerstone of central European cuisine. Our version isn't as involved as some recipes since it doesn't call for any special fermentation processes, but it is an effective substitute. We cheat a little bit by adding vinegar to the brine. We ferment all types of vegetables in the restaurant's basement using this method, and it works great with Brussels sprouts and Chinese cabbages as well.

The speed at which sauerkraut will ferment is based on ambient temperature: the hotter the room, the quicker the fermentation. This is a traditional preservation method, so the sauerkraut will keep well for a very long time in your refrigerator.

5 pounds green cabbage, cored and thinly sliced

3 cups peeled, shredded carrots

3 cups thinly sliced red onion

1 cup apple cider vinegar

3 tablespoons sea salt

3 tablespoons mustard powder

1/2 cup chopped flat leaf parsley

1/2 cup toasted caraway seeds

In a large nonreactive mixing bowl, combine the cabbage, carrots, onion, vinegar, salt, mustard powder, parsley and caraway seed. Mix well. Transfer to a large container and weight it with a heavy plate, making sure to press down firmly. Cover the kraut with cheesecloth tied tightly with butcher's twine. (Alternately, cover with a lid if it fits tightly on the container.)

Check the kraut after 24 hours as the brine begins to build. Every day or two, "burp" the kraut to release the carbon dioxide that builds during fermentation. Press down hard on the plate during this process to help push the water out of the vegetables.

After about a week, a bloom will appear on the surface of the brine. Don't be concerned, as this is a natural process. The kraut is under the anaerobic protection of the brine. Simply remove the plate and rinse it. The bloom may be skimmed from the top. Return the plate to the container if needed to keep the kraut fully submerged. Taste the kraut periodically until the flavor fully develops, and the vegetables are tender. Transfer to quart jars, cover and refrigerate.

# BLACK PEPPER DRESSING

There are only a few ingredients in this simple sour cream-based dressing, so their quality is important. Use a natural sour cream, free of stabilizers, as well as good buttermilk. This dressing has enough flavor to stand up to heartier dark greens such as kale and chicories. Use the best grade of peppercorn you can find—preferably Tellicherry—since it takes center stage.

2 cups sour cream

1/2 cup buttermilk

1/2 cup grapeseed or sunflower oil

2 teaspoons sea salt

1 tablespoon freshly ground black pepper

In a medium bowl, whisk together the sour cream, buttermilk, grapeseed oil, salt and pepper.

Transfer to a container with a tight lid and refrigerate. Use within 7 days.

# TOMATO ROSEMARY DRESSING

MAKES ABOUT 2½ CUPS

Years ago, I created a vegetarian paella dish that called for filets of Roma tomatoes. To make the filets, we cut off the tops and bottoms of the tomatoes and removed the hearts. While I was pleased with the positive reception to the paella, we found ourselves with a surplus of tomato hearts. Thus Tomato Rosemary Dressing was created.

The acid from the tomatoes replaces the vinegar, so the dressing isn't technically a vinaigrette. But it's delicious, especially on a mix of seasonal garden greens. In keeping with Heartland's style, I use grapeseed oil, but I think this is even better with high-quality extra virgin olive oil. Note that it takes about 2 cups of tomato hearts puréed and strained of seeds to produce 1 cup of purée. Reserve the filets to toss into salad or pasta.

2 teaspoons sea salt

I cup seedless, skinless tomato purée

2 tablespoons chopped garlic

I tablespoon chopped shallots

2 tablespoons chopped rosemary

I teaspoon freshly ground black pepper

I½ cups grapeseed oil or high-quality extra virgin olive oil

In a blender, dissolve the salt in the tomato purée. Add garlic, shallots, rosemary and pepper. Working on high speed, slowly add the oil in a thin stream until fully incorporated. Transfer to jars, cover tightly and refrigerate for up to 2 weeks.

# APPLE CIDER–WALNUT OIL VINAIGRETTE

MAKES ABOUT 2 CUPS

As summer begins to wane and we move into hardier greens and late fruits, I find that we need salad dressings more in tune with the season. This one hits just the right notes. The key to balancing the flavors is tempering the walnut oil and apple cider vinegar with grapeseed oil and fresh apple cider. Otherwise, the vinaigrette is too strong for even a robust combination of greens.

Be aware that salt does not dissolve in fat. To ensure that the salt is well distributed in your dressing, dissolve it first in the acid ingredient, such as lemon juice, tomato purée or vinegar.

| | |
|---|---|
| 2 teaspoons sea salt | 2 tablespoons chopped Italian parsley |
| ³/₄ cup apple cider vinegar | 1 teaspoon freshly ground black pepper |
| ¹/₄ cup fresh apple cider | |
| 2 tablespoons chopped garlic | ³/₄ cup grapeseed oil |
| 1 tablespoon chopped shallots | ¹/₄ cup walnut oil |

In a blender, dissolve the salt in the vinegar and cider. Add the garlic, shallots, parsley and pepper. Working on high speed, slowly add the oils in a thin stream until fully incorporated. Transfer to jars, cover and refrigerate until ready to serve.

## VARIATION ON A THEME

For **Pancetta Vinaigrette**, substitute 1 cup freshly squeezed lemon juice for the apple cider vinegar and apple cider. Omit the walnut oil and increase grapeseed or olive oil to 1 cup. Once the dressing has been fully incorporated, add ¹/₂ cup crumbled crisply cooked pancetta. This vinaigrette is especially nice warmed and served over a strongly-flavored vegetable like Brussels sprouts (see page 132). Makes 2¹/₂ cups.

# RHUBARB CHUTNEY

We have made chutney with virtually every local fruit, from fresh cherries in midsummer to apples and cranberries in the fall to prunes in the dead of winter. I especially like rhubarb (technically not a fruit, but a vegetable), both on its own or in combination with strawberries or another summer fruit. I even make one version with toasted walnuts in place of fresh fruit; I stir the walnuts into the chutney after the syrup has finished cooking, to help preserve their crunchy texture. Aside from that, the composition of the chutney does not change, even though the main ingredient might.

| | |
|---|---|
| 1¹/2 cups apple cider vinegar | 2 garlic cloves, chopped |
| 2¹/2 pounds rhubarb, cut into 1-inch pieces (other fresh or preserved fruit such as cherries or prunes may be substituted) | 1 medium sweet onion, chopped |
| | 1 cinnamon stick |
| | 1 teaspoon brown mustard seed |
| 3 jalapeño peppers, seeded and minced | 1 teaspoon grated fresh ginger |
| | ¹/4 teaspoon ground allspice |
| ¹/2 cup golden raisins | Pinch ground cloves |
| ¹/2 cup dried currants | 1 teaspoon sea salt |
| 1¹/2 cups light brown sugar, packed | 1 bay leaf |

Bring the vinegar to a boil in a nonreactive pot. Reduce the heat to moderately low and add the rhubarb. Simmer for 5 minutes. Add the jalapeños, raisins, currants, brown sugar, garlic, onion, cinnamon, mustard seed, ginger, allspice, cloves, salt and bay leaf. Simmer until the chutney thickens, about 25 minutes. Remove the bay leaf and cinnamon stick.

Spoon into clean jars, and cover tightly. The chutney may be served warm, cold or at room temperature. It will keep for 2 weeks in the refrigerator.

## VARIATION ON A THEME

For **Cranberry-Apple Chutney**, substitute 2¹/2 pounds combined fresh cranberries, chopped apples and preserved cranberries in place of the rhubarb. Replace the brown sugar with 1 ¹/2 cups wildflower honey.

# PUMPKIN SEED PARSLEY PISTOU

MAKES ABOUT ¾ CUP

You say pesto, I say pistou. Well, okay—I say both. Pesto is a traditional Ligurian sauce of basil, garlic, salt, olive oil, pine nuts and Parmesan cheese. But pesto is also a fairly generic term for any sauce made from ingredients that are pounded, crushed and served uncooked. The name is derived from the mortar and pestle used to pound the sauce. Pistou, the Provençal version, eliminates pine nuts and cheese and is most commonly stirred into vegetable soups for a fresh, herbal contrast.

Since Heartland cuisine is based on Italian and French techniques with local and regional ingredients, I'm comfortable serving both pesto and pistou. For a Midwestern interpretation, I substitute parsley for basil, grapeseed oil for olive and enrich it with my favorite locally harvested pumpkin or sunflower seeds. Freshly cracked pepper is essential. This interpretation offers greater flexibility for pairing the sauce with pasta and soups, and makes a delightful accompaniment to simply grilled fish.

I large garlic clove

½ teaspoon sea salt

3½ tablespoons grapeseed oil

¼ cup lightly toasted pumpkin or sunflower seeds

I cup chopped parsley leaves

I tablespoon freshly squeezed lemon juice

¼ teaspoon freshly ground black pepper

Using a food processor or (preferably) a mortar and pestle, crush the garlic with the salt to form a smooth paste. Add the oil and seeds, and crush until they are well incorporated. Add the parsley and process or pound until loosely incorporated. Season to taste with the lemon juice and black pepper. The pistou can be stored in your refrigerator or freezer until needed.

## VARIATION ON A THEME

For **Hazelnut Parsley Pistou**, substitute ¼ cup lightly toasted hazelnuts for the pumpkin seeds.

# WALNUT BASIL PESTO

In Heartland's menu lexicon, adding grated Wisconsin Parmesan cheese transforms pistou into pesto. Substituting meaty local walnuts for the typical pine nuts makes this a uniquely Midwestern sauce.

1 large garlic clove

1/2 teaspoon sea salt

3 1/2 tablespoons grapeseed oil

1/4 cup lightly toasted walnuts

1 cup fresh basil leaves, chopped

1 tablespoon freshly squeezed lemon juice

1/4 teaspoon freshly ground black pepper

1/4 cup grated Parmesan cheese

Using a food processor or (preferably) a mortar and pestle, crush the garlic with the salt to form a smooth paste. Add the oil and walnuts, and crush until they are well incorporated. Add the basil and process or pound until loosely incorporated. Season to taste with the lemon juice and black pepper. Stir in the grated cheese before serving. The pistou may be refrigerated or frozen for up to 2 months.

# PRESERVED TOMATO PESTO

MAKES ABOUT 1½ CUPS

This pesto is best made in a food processor, since the dried tomatoes require more power to puree them than the sweat of your brow and the force of your hand. The sauce can be refrigerated, but if you intend to freeze it, do so before adding the Parmesan, since the milk solids in the cheese tend to separate when frozen.

Of course, we use our own dehydrated tomatoes, but feel free to use store-bought sun-dried tomatoes. To reconstitute them, simply heat some water just short of boiling and pour over the tomatoes. Let them soak for about 5 minutes, then drain and pat dry before continuing with the recipe. This pesto is great on crostini or as a sauce for pasta.

½ teaspoon sea salt

I teaspoon freshly squeezed lemon juice

I cup sun-dried tomatoes, reconstituted

I cup fresh basil leaves

3 tablespoons grapeseed oil

2 tablespoons walnuts, lightly toasted

I large garlic clove

¼ cup grated Parmesan cheese

¼ teaspoon freshly ground black pepper

In the bowl of a food processor, combine the salt and lemon juice. Add the tomatoes, basil, oil, walnuts, garlic, Parmesan and pepper, and process into a fine paste. Transfer to a clean jar, cover tightly and refrigerate until needed.

# CHICKEN STOCK

There is a good reason why the French refer to stocks as *fonds*. They are literally the foundations of many essential sauces and soups. I often use a skyscraper as a metaphor. We can build the tallest, most beautiful skyscraper ever seen, but if the foundation cannot support it, it will tumble to the ground. In other words, without a strong foundation, your sauces and soups will be weak. Lerning how to prepare a proper stock is essential to becoming a really good cook, and for the home cook, it's a simple, satisfying craft.

Over the years, I have established a basic method, so most of my stocks are made in basically the same way aside from the bouquet garni and the cooking time. Each type of stock benefits from the use of different aromatics, and I have worked at perfecting those combinations through years of trial and error. In addition, certain proteins do not benefit from long cooking times as they tend to get bitter, while others require much more time.

Another technique I use is repetition. When preparing a reduction utilizing a certain type of stock, I often repeat the bouquet garni which helps to emphasize and enhance the flavors I am seeking to present.

10 pounds chicken carcasses

2 white onions, peeled and diced

3 carrots, peeled and diced

1/2 stalk celery diced

1 garlic bulb, quartered

1 cup red wine

Bouquet garni (2 thyme sprigs, 2 parsley sprigs, 2 sage sprigs, 1 bay leaf, 10 black peppercorns)

1/2 cup tomato concentrate

Preheat the oven to 350°. Chop the carcasses and distribute them evenly in a roasting pan. Roast until well browned, about 30 minutes.

Transfer the carcasses to a large stockpot along with the onions, carrots, celery and garlic. Skim off and discard any fat that has accumulated in the roasting pan, and add the red wine. Place the pan over moderately low heat and deglaze, scraping to incorporate roasted bits from the bottom.

Pour the wine into the stockpot and add the bouquet garni, making sure it is fully submerged in the liquid. Add the tomato concentrate and enough water to just cover the bones. Bring to a boil, then reduce to a simmer. Keep skimming the surface of the stock as it cooks, about 4 hours. Strain the stock through a fine-mesh sieve lined with moistened cheesecloth. Transfer the stock to containers, cover tightly and refrigerate or freeze.

# COURT-BOUILLON

This is the ultimate elegantly simple vegetable stock. Court-bouillon translates from French as "short broth." It refers to the cooking time, which generally does not exceed one hour. You may try cooking yours a little longer if you prefer a richer, more concentrated broth. This is the base for so many recipes—a workhorse of the kitchen.

2 tablespoons grapeseed oil

2 white onions, peeled and diced

3 carrots, peeled and diced

1/2 stalk of celery, diced

I leek, diced

I garlic bulb, quartered

I cup dry white wine

Bouquet garni (2 thyme sprigs, 2 marjoram sprigs, 3 parsley sprigs, I bay leaf, 5 whole allspice, 10 white peppercorns, 10 black peppercorns, 12 fennel seeds)

Warm the grapeseed oil in a stockpot over moderate heat. Add the onions, carrots, celery, leek and garlic and sweat until tender, about 10 minutes. Add the white wine, bouquet garni and 4 quarts of cold water. Bring to a boil over high heat. Reduce the heat and simmer for 1½ to 2 hours, skimming occasionally.

Strain the stock through a fine-mesh sieve lined with moistened cheesecloth. Transfer the stock to containers, cover tightly and refrigerate or freeze.

# BROWN VEAL STOCK

A classic building block of French cuisine, veal stock plays many roles in the kitchen. Use it to enhance stews and sauces, reduce it to a syrupy elixir for Glace de Viande (page 270) or simply sip it from a mug to enjoy the robust goodness of a soup brewed from the bones of well-raised animals. We're never without it in the Heartland kitchen.

10 pounds veal bones

1/2 pound white onions, peeled and chopped

1/2 pound carrots, peeled and chopped

1/2 pound celery chopped

4 garlic cloves

1/2 cup red wine

Bouquet garni (3 thyme sprigs, 1/4 bunch parsley, 3 marjoram sprigs, 1 bay leaf and 20 black peppercorns)

1/2 cup tomato concentrate

Preheat the oven to 350°F. Distribute the bones evenly in a roasting pan. Roast until well browned, about 30 minutes.

Transfer the bones to a large stockpot with the onions, carrots, celery and garlic. Spoon off any fat that has accumulated in the bottom of the roasting pan and deglaze the pan with the red wine over moderate heat, making sure to scrape any roasted bits from the bottom of the pan.

Pour the wine into the stockpot and add the bouquet garni, making sure it is submerged to ensure proper diffusion of the herbs and spices during cooking. Add the tomato concentrate and enough water to just cover the bones, about 5 quarts. Bring to a boil, then reduce to a simmer. Keep skimming the surface of the stock as it cooks for about 8 hours. Strain through a fine-mesh sieve lined with moistened cheesecloth.

# GLACE DE VIANDE

Glace de viande is French for meat glaze, and the method that follows is the same for any meat stock that is reduced to a glaze. The only thing that changes is the aromatics in the bouquet garni, which are determined by the type of meat stock used.

Unlike demiglace, which is half way to reaching a glaze, glace de viande is fully reduced and is the culinary equivalent of liquid gold. I have calculated that it costs our kitchen $200 to produce one gallon of glace de viande.

A little glace goes a long way, so be judicious when using it in your sauces. It also freezes well, so filling up an ice cube tray is a clever and efficient way to store it for future use. Store the frozen stock cubes in a zippered freezer bag.

¹/2 cup red wine

1 bouquet garni (10 black peppercorns, 3 thyme sprigs, 1 bay leaf, 1 peeled shallots and 3 garlic cloves)

4 quarts Brown Veal Stock (page 269)

Pour the wine into a large, nonreactive saucepan and add the bouquet garni. Bring to a boil over high heat, and cook until the wine has reduced by half. Add the stock and return to a boil.

Reduce the heat to moderately low, and simmer until the stock has reduced by three quarters of its volume, making sure to periodically skim the top. Discard the bouquet garni, and strain the glace through a fine-mesh sieve lined with moistened cheesecloth. Chill in an ice bath. Transfer to containers, cover and refrigerate or freeze.

# FISH FUMET

Taking the time to learn how to prepare a proper stock is essential to becoming a good home cook. This versatile fish stock makes all the difference between a so-so dish and one that really sings.

¼ cup grapeseed oil

10 pounds fish heads and bones (from mild white-fleshed fish)

½ pound white onions, peeled and chopped

½ pound carrots, peeled and chopped

½ pound celery chopped

½ pound leek tops, chopped

½ pound fennel tops, chopped

1 garlic bulb, quartered

1 cup dry white wine

Bouquet garni (2 thyme sprigs, 2 parsley sprigs, 2 tarragon sprigs, 1 bay leaf, 5 whole allspice, 2 whole nutmeg, 20 black peppercorns, 20 white peppercorns)

In a large stockpot, warm the oil over moderate heat. Add the fish heads and bones, onions, carrots, celery, leek, fennel and garlic and cook until the vegetables are tender, about 10 minutes. Add the wine and bouquet garni, making sure to push the bouquet under the vegetables to ensure proper diffusion of the aromatics.

Add enough water to just cover the ingredients. Bring to a boil over high heat. Reduce the heat to low and simmer for 2 hours, occasionally skimming impurities from the surface of the stock. Strain through a fine-mesh sieve lined with moistened cheesecloth. Transfer to containers, cover tightly and refrigerate or freeze.

# CRAYFISH STOCK

In other parts of the country, lobster shells make a worthy substitute for our freshwater crayfish bodies. For us in the Midwest, this stock is a true taste of the terroir.

2 tablespoons grapeseed oil

5 pounds raw crayfish bodies

1 1/2 teaspoons paprika

1/2 teaspoon cayenne pepper

1/4 cup tomato concentrate

1/4 pound onions, peeled and chopped

1/4 pound carrots, peeled and chopped

1/4 pound celery chopped

1/4 pound leek greens, chopped

1/4 pound fennel tops, chopped

6 garlic cloves, smashed

1/2 cup white wine

1/4 cup brandy

Bouquet garni (1 thyme sprig, 1 parsley sprig, 1 tarragon sprig, 1 bay leaf, 2 whole allspice, 1 whole nutmegs, 10 black peppercorns, 10 white peppercorns)

Heat the grapeseed oil in a large, heavy pot over moderate heat. Add the crayfish bodies, paprika, cayenne pepper and tomato. Cook for about 10 minutes, just until the crayfish turn red. Using a meat mallet, crush the crayfish bodies. Add the onions, carrots, celery, leek greens, fennel and garlic, and cook for about 5 minutes, until just tender. Deglaze with the wine and brandy. Add the bouquet garni making sure to push it under the vegetables to ensure proper diffusion of the herbs and spices during cooking.

Add enough water to just cover the ingredients and bring to a boil. Reduce the heat to a simmer and cook for 2 hours. Take the time to frequently skim any oil and albumen from the surface of the stock.

Strain the stock through a colander, pressing the crayfish with a meat mallet in order to recover all of the juices. Strain again through a fine-mesh sieve lined with moistened cheesecloth. Chill in an ice bath, transfer to containers, cover and refrigerate or freeze.

# MUSHROOM BROTH

This broth was born out of necessity. Professional kitchens usually have a surplus of stems and trimmings from both cultivated and wild mushrooms. Consequently, I call for mushroom stems, but you may use coarsely chopped button or crimini mushrooms in the absence of a pile of stems. I leave it unseasoned because we often use this as a poaching liquid or to enrich sauces. It's also great on its own, so season it when appropriate. I prefer white pepper over black so there are no visible specks floating around in the broth.

2 tablespoons grapeseed oil

2¹/2 pounds mushrooms, stems and trimmings included

¹/2 pound white onions, peeled and chopped

¹/2 pound carrots, peeled and chopped

¹/2 pound celery chopped

6 garlic bulbs, quartered

¹/2 cup sherry

Bouquet garni (2 thyme sprigs, I parsley sprig, Ibay leaf, 7 black peppercorns)

Warm the oil in a large stockpot over moderate heat. Add the mushrooms, onions, carrots, celery and garlic and sweat for 5 minutes until tender but not browned. Add the sherry and the bouquet garni, making sure to push the bouquet under the vegetables for proper diffusion of the aromatics.

Add enough water to just cover the vegetables and bring to a boil. Reduce the heat to low and simmer for 2 hours, frequently skimming impurities from the surface with a large spoon.

Strain the broth through a fine-mesh sieve lined with moistened cheesecloth. Discard the bouquet garni. Allow the broth to cool, then transfer to containers, cover tightly and refrigerate for up to 1 week or freeze.

# CORN BROTH

The Midwest is corn country, especially Minnesota, Iowa and Nebraska. This is a recipe that uses corn cobs, a byproduct always in great abundance during harvest season. After slicing off the corn kernels, we store the cobs until we have enough to make this broth. As with mushroom broth, I leave it unseasoned so that it can be used in a number of ways. We often use it as a soup base for chowders, and we have even clarified it to serve as a delicate consommé.

2 tablespoons grapeseed oil

2½ pounds onions, peeled and chopped

2½ pounds carrots, peeled and chopped

2½ pounds celery, chopped

1 pound leek greens, chopped

1 pound fennel tops, chopped

1 garlic bulb, quartered

10 corn cobs

2 cups white wine

Bouquet garni (3 thyme sprigs, ¼ bunch parsley, 3 tarragon sprigs, 1 bay leaf, 5 whole allspice, 1 whole nutmeg, 10 black peppercorns, 10 white peppercorns)

Heat the oil in a large stockpot over moderately high heat. Add the onions, carrots, celery, leeks, fennel and garlic and sweat until tender but not browned, about 5 minutes. Add the corn cobs, wine and bouquet garni, making sure to push the bouquet under the vegetables to ensure proper diffusion of the aromatics.

Add enough water to just cover the vegetables. Bring to a boil over high heat. Reduce the heat to a simmer and cook for 2 hours, frequently skimming any oil from the surface. Strain through a fine mesh-sieve lined with moistened cheesecloth. Discard the bouquet garni. Transfer to containers, cover tightly and refrigerate.

# THE ART OF GEORGE MORRISON

(1919-2000)

The Heartland's rhythms, vistas and geometry inspired the Ojibwe abstract expressionist George Morrison. He studied art in 1950's New York and taught at Rhode Island School of Design, but made his last home in Grand Portage, Minnesota, not far from the place where he was born.

**Red Cube**
1983, lithograph, 29⁷⁄₈ x 22¹⁄₂ in.

**Untitled (Quarry Face)**
1949, pencil, pastel, and ink on paper, 18 x 24 in.

**Untitled (Black on Mustard Yellow)**
1974, ink and pencil on paper, 9³⁄₄ x 13¹⁄₄ in.

**Brown and Black Textured Squares**
1982, ink on paper, 12³⁄₈ x 9¹⁄₄ in.

*All works are in the permanent collection of
the Minnesota Museum of American Art*

**Cumulated Landscape**
1976, wood, 48 x 120 x 3 in.

**Provincetown, Sky-Seascape**
1970, found wood, 8 x 11 in.

**Quiet Light Towards Evening, Red Rock Variation: Lake Superior Landscape**
1990, acrylic and pastel on paper, 22½ x 30⅛ in.

**Untitled**
1977, ink and pencil on paper, 41³/₈ x 30 in.

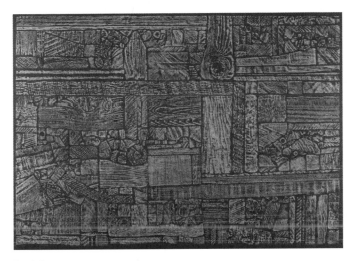

**Untitled**
1978, lithograph, 30 x 44½ in.

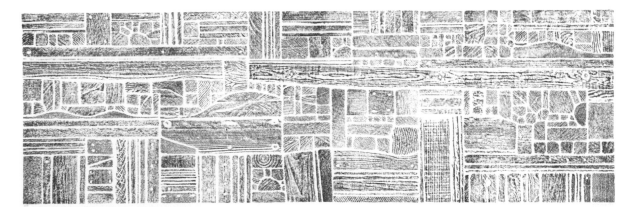

**Untitled**
1987, lithograph, 25⁵/₈ x 71³/₈ in.

# ACKNOWLEDGEMENTS

I have many people to thank for their help in creating this book. First, my good friends and fellow Minnesotans, Lynne Rossetto Kasper and Andrew Zimmern, who were kind enough to contribute their comments. Like Lynne, my wife and I reside in St. Paul, "America's Most Livable City." While Andrew and his family have relocated across the river to Minneapolis, also known as the "lesser twin," we try not to hold that against him.

My former sous chef Alan Bergo not only tested many of the recipes in this book, but also styled most of the photographs. That brings me to Tom Thulen, the supremely talented photographer whose vison and work so aptly captured the spirit of my food and the sources of its origins. My good friend Thom Middlebrook offered encouragement while navigating for Tom and me as we traveled from farm to farm visiting and taking photographs. While his navigation skills leave much to be desired, Thom's good humor and enthusiasm were invaluable during those long days on the road. I must also thank the proprietors and denizens of the many farms, dairies and ranches that supply Heartland with the wonderful ingredients I am so privileged to cook with. They are truly the inspiration for what I do.

Thanks to my hardworking, dedicated Heartland team in both the front and back of house, many of whom have labored side by side with me for the last thirteen years. A special thanks goes out to sous chefs Amy "Peanut" Buckmeier and Brandon "Brando" Randolph and their culinary brigade: Tater Tot, Shlomo, Satan and Dan, as well as longtime pastry chef Jack Fulton, who helped me formulate the dessert recipes and without whom I would have been lost.

I'd like to thank Mayor Chris Coleman and the city of St. Paul, especially the neighborhoods of Macalester-Groveland and Lowertown, for welcoming us into their community, as well the many loyal patrons who have supported our efforts all these years. Our business partners, Bob Cornelius and the dear departed Sandra Cornelius, first proposed our restaurant and made it possible for us to begin this journey with the original fifty-seat incarnation that was Heartland in Macalester-Groveland, and the inimitable Kris Maritz asked us to partner with her to create the new Heartland in Lowertown. She was instrumental in helping us grow to more than 400 seats housed in roughly 25,000 square feet of converted warehouse space across the street from the glorious St. Paul Farmers Market.

My most cherished thanks go to my beautiful, intelligent and hardworking wife Mega Hoehn, who not only allowed me to pursue what eventually became Heartland, but also provided friendship and moral support when times were tough. She is the product of two wonderful parents, Laurrie and Gary Hoehn. Gary handcrafted much of the interior of the original Heartland and is still there for us as we continually transform the restaurant. Without them, this book would likely have never been written.

Speaking of family, I would be remiss not mention my own crazy Italian relatives, especially my parents and grandparents, who instilled in me at a very early age a profound appreciation for good food. A deep measure of gratitude goes out to Kristin Makholm of the Minnesota Museum of American Art, and especially Briand Morrison. With Kristin's assistance, we were able to secure Briand's permission to include in this book and on the cover the extraordinary artwork of his renowned father, the Ojibwe artist George Morrison. Finally, I must thank all the talented chefs, culinarians, artisans, designers, scientists and craftspeople with whom I have had the extreme pleasure of working over the last forty years. Their guidance, inspiration and leadership have helped shaped my vision. It is my profound hope that I have been able to do them justice.

# INDEX